ILLUSTRATED HISTORY OF THE VIETNAM WAR CARRIER OPERATIONS

BANTAM BOOKS

TORONTO • NEW YORK • LONDON • SYDNEY • AUCKLAND

CARRIER OPERATIONS

by

Edward J. Marolda

YANKEE TEAM

At a point 100 miles northeast of Da
Nang support carrier *Intrepid* steams
through the South China Sea while
nearby on the flight deck of the
nuclear-powered *Enterprise* red-shirted
ordnancemen ready A-7E Corsair II
and A-6 Intruder attack planes for
operations over North Vietnam.

RESUPPLY AT SEA

A UH-46 Sea Knight helicopter delivers aircraft fuel tanks to carrier *Hancock* . by the ''vertical replenishment'' method as fast combat support ship *Sacramento* pumps fuel to the flattop through connecting hoselines. This underway replenishment of fuel, ammunition, provisions and equipment enabled the fleet to remain on station in the Gulf of Tonkin throughout the Vietnam War.

CATAPULTS AWAY

The view from *Hancock*'s bridge as an F-8 Crusader fighter prepares for launching in the clear Souteast Asian sky. Flight deck personnel stand by to ready other aircraft for takeoff. Units from this attack carrier conducted operations in Laos and South Vietnam during 1970 and 1971.

EDITORS: Richard Grant, Richard Ballantine. PHOTO RESEARCH: John Moore.
DRAWINGS: John Batchelor. MAPS: Peter Williams. STUDIO: Kim Williams.
PRODUCED BY: The Up & Coming Publishing Company, Bearsville, New York.

CARRIER OPERATIONS
THE ILLUSTRATED HISTORY OF THE VIETNAM WAR
A Bantam Book/ August 1987

ACKNOWLEDGEMENTS

*The author is deeply grateful to Captain Rosario Rausa, USN, and
Roy Grossnick of the Naval Historical Center's Aviation History Branch for
their perceptive and thorough critique of the work. Equally deserving of
praise is Mrs Vincetta Dallmann, who skilfully and diligently repaired the
draft manuscript for publication. Special thanks also must go to my wife,
Beverly, and our sons Jeff, Brian and Michael for bearing with an absent-
minded historian as he devoted his full energies to researching and writing
this book.*

*Photographs for this book were selected from the archives of DAVA and
Military Archive Research Services*

Library of Congress Cataloging-in-Publication Data

Marolda, Edward J.
Carrier operations.
(The Illustrated history of the Vietnam War)
Bibliography: p. 157
1. Vietnamese Conflict, 1961-1975—Aerial operations,
American. 2. Aircraft carriers—United States.
I. Title. II. Series.
DS558.8.M3 1987   959.704'348   87-11544
ISBN 0-553-34348-3

Published simultaneously in the United States and Canada

PRINTED IN THE UNITED STATES OF AMERICA

CW   0   9   8   7   6   5   4   3   2   1

Contents

Turning Point

The Gulf of Tonkin Incident

NINETEEN SIXTY-FOUR marked a turning point in the long struggle for Vietnam. For, despite the flood of American advisors, aircraft, ships and craft, vehicles, weapons, and supplies pouring into Vietnam between 1962 and 1964, the South Vietnamese military was losing the fight. The Viet Cong in South Vietnam controlled more and more of the countryside as they decimated Saigon's forces. The prospects for the government's survival were even more dismal. After the ousting and assassination of the long-serving President Ngo Dinh Diem in 1963, one regime followed another. The Don-Minh-Kim junta that deposed Diem was replaced by General Nguyen Khanh, a politically ambitious officer of modest talents and little popular appeal.

The participation of American military units in combined operations with the South Vietnamese, such as the US helicopter transportation of government troops and the anti-infiltration coastal patrol, only retarded the enemy's progress. At this level of assistance, the anti-communist effort in South Vietnam was doomed.

In keeping with the strategy of "flexible response," then the favored American approach to communist aggression, even stronger US military countermeasures were needed. But the Johnson administration, which replaced the Kennedy government after the assassination of the president in November 1963, decided to act rather than react to communist moves. Washington pursued a strategy of "graduated military pressure" against North Vietnam to convince the Ho Chi Minh regime that further support of the Viet Cong in the South was a dangerous policy to follow. This meant taking

armed action against the communists outside of
South Vietnam. In particular, it meant strikes
against targets in Laos, through which passed the
vital Ho Chi Minh Trail, the main supply line to the
South, and North Vietnam, nerve center of the campaign to unify Vietnam.

President Lyndon B. Johnson's principal
assistants, including Secretary of Defense Robert
McNamara, presidential advisor McGeorge Bundy,
and the Joint Chiefs of Staff (JCS) felt that when

SHOW-OF-FORCE: Bird's eye view of the 4½-acre deck of the *Kitty Hawk*. In April 1964 it lead a deterrent task force into the Gulf of Tonkin. Commissioned in 1961, *Kitty Hawk* was one of a new generation of super-Forrestal-class carriers capable of operating up to 90 aircraft. The angled deck design made it possible to maneuver and park more aircraft. It also made landings less hazardous. When a pilot missed the arresting wire, he added power and went round again for a second attempt.

he United States had tightened the thumbscrews ufficiently on the North Vietnamese, they would give up their aggressive program.

Top naval leaders also believed that the North Vietnamese would back down in the face of American naval and air power, as the communists had in the Lebanon and Taiwan Strait crises of 1958, n the extended confrontation over Laos from 1959 o 1962, and in the Cuban missile crisis. Admirals George W. Anderson and David L. McDonald, suc-

Adm. George W. Anderson, Jr., —Chief of Naval Operations 1961-1963. As early as 1962 he called for a campaign of harrassment against North Vietnam to deter it from supporting the Viet Cong.

cessive Chiefs of Naval Operations, Admiral Claude V. Ricketts, the forceful Vice Chief of Naval Operations, and Admiral Harry D. Felt, the commander of all US forces in the Pacific, among others, pushed hard for military measures against the North Vietnamese.

This began in February 1964 when South Vietnamese commando teams—trained, armed, and directed by the US Military Assistance Command, Vietnam (MACV) in South Vietnam—were infiltrated into the North to conduct sabotage. This was operation 34A.

In April, US leaders positioned aircraft carrier *Kitty Hawk* and her escorts at the entrance to the Gulf of Tonkin. This operating area, 100 miles off the Indochinese coast at 16 degrees north latitude, 110 degrees east longitude, soon became known as Yankee Station.

This show of force also resulted from developments in Laos, where the North Vietnamese and the Laotian communist guerillas, the Pathet Lao, had opened an offensive against Laotian government troops. The communist objective was to clear hostile forces from the area so that the Ho Chi Minh Trail could be used more effectively to pump men and supplies into South Vietnam.

Laotian Prime Minister Souvanna Phouma, who was allied with the anti-communist elements in Laos, called for US military aid. Of more significance, he authorized American military aircraft to carry out low-level reconnaissance in eastern Laos.

Quickly seizing this opportunity, on May 17, 1964 Washington directed the Commander in Chief Pacific, (CINCPAC) to begin an aerial reconnaissance and show-of-force operation, called Yankee Team, with US Navy and US Air Force units. The Air Force 2nd Air Division, based at Saigon's Tan Son Nhut airfield, flew the first Yankee Team mission two days later. Then, on May 21, Rear Admiral William F. Bringle's *Kitty Hawk* task group, which also included destroyer *Maddox* launched two RF-8A Crusader photo reconnaissance planes for the operation. The Light Photographic Squadron (VFP) 63 aircraft passed low over the Plain of Jars in central Laos looking for communist road traffic. They photographed the beehive activ-

y below. Then, over Xieng Khouang, ground fire
suddenly punched holes in one of the Crusaders. The
plane's port wing caught fire and burned for 20
minutes as the pilot headed for *Kitty Hawk* under
the protection of his wingman. Both aircraft landed
safely.

Kitty Hawk's Carrier Air Wing 11 was speedily
reinforced with reconnaissance units. Seven RF-8As
flew in from *Bon Homme Richard* at Subic Bay in
the Philippines and from a Marine shore-based unit,
and two RA-3B Skywarriors came from Cubi Point.
Then, on June 6, *Constellation* and her "photo recce"
aircraft joined the ships off South Vietnam.

Between May 21 and June 9, the Yankee Team
flew over 130 missions into Laos. The Navy usually
concentrated on the routes from the Plain of Jars
eastward to North Vietnam while the Air Force
overflew the Laotian panhandle south of Nape Pass.
Communist guns hit a number of aircraft, but
failed to bring any down.

This good fortune ended on June 6, 1964, when the
US Navy lost its first pilot and plane in Vietnam.
Lieutenant Charles F. Klusmann and his wingman,
Lieutenant Jerry Kuechmann, of *Kitty Hawk*'s VFP
63, flew their RF-8As over Laotian Route 7. This
road was the main supply artery from North Vietnam into the Plain of Jars. Naval aviators called the

**Adm. Harry
D. Felt
—commanded
US forces in
the Pacific
during the
build-up to
war.**

**ON THE DOORSTEP:
Sited 100 miles
east of Da
Nang at 16
degrees north
latitude and
110 degrees
east longitude,
Yankee Station
was the
principal
operational
location for
carrier-based
aircraft
operating
against North
Vietnam.
Over half the
bombing raids
launched
against the
north came
from Yankee
Station.**

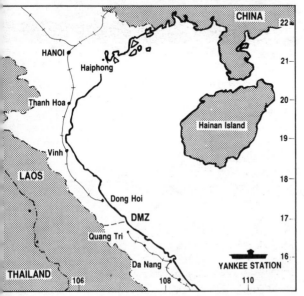

Turning Point

JUST A PATCH OF OCEAN:

Early in 1965, the ships of the Seventh Fleet's Task Force 77 assembled on Yankee Station—a patch of ocean defined by map coordinates. Here, flanked by a cruiser and a screen of destroyers, *Ranger*, *Hancock*, *Coral Sea*, and *Yorktown* ready their 300 aircraft for combat. These could be over North Vietnam within minutes of receiving a hurry call. Carriers were claimed to provide better security than land airstrips but that did not prevent unwelcome Soviet spy trawlers (inset) snooping.

19

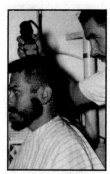

Close shave —Lt. Charles F. Klusmann gets his first haircut in three months after escaping from a Laotian prison camp. Klusman's RF-8A Crusader was raked with 37mm antiaircaft fire and he had to bail out from the stricken Crusader. His was the first Navy plane to be shot down in the Vietnam War.

stretch between Khang Khay and Ban Ban "lead alley" because it was lined with antiaircraft guns.

Trying to get the best pictures, Klusmann flew his Crusader low. This dedication to duty was dangerous. On one pass, a 37-millimeter gun raked his plane. The young lieutenant struggled to keep the RF-8A in the air, but northwest of Xieng Khouang all systems failed. He bailed out of the stricken aircraft and floated to earth. A hail of small arms fire followed Klusmann down but missed him.

Meanwhile, wingman Jerry Kuechmann called in recovery aircraft. Helicopters tried to reach the downed aviator but heavy ground fire made it impossible. American flak suppression aircraft were too far away. The Pathet Lao guerrillas soon converged on Klusmann's position and captured him.

The lessons of this first search and rescue (SAR) attempt were not lost on the carrier aviators. In future missions, supporting aircraft were kept close at hand and ready to swoop in on the enemy. Usually they were the old reliable, propeller-driven A-1H Skyraiders, able to stay aloft for long periods and carry a heavy load.

While his comrades were improving SAR procedures, Klusmann was forced by his captors to hobble through the steamy, insect-ridden jungle to a prisoner of war (POW) compound near Khang Khay. There, the communists threw him into solitary confinement, denied him medical attention and sufficient food, and worked on his mind. Finally, injured, weak from hunger, and alone, Klusmann was forced to sign a written statement condemning US policy in Southeast Asia.

The young naval aviator did not give up. When the Pathet Lao moved him to another, less closely guarded camp, he attempted to escape. He failed on this first try, but a short time later, the lieutenant and five Laotian and Thai prisoners burrowed under the wall of their hut and slipped past the guards into the jungle. Three of the men disappeared soon afterward when the group separated to avoid a communist patrol. Another prisoner, throwing caution to the wind, walked into a village to get food; it was enemy held. The man was last seen being led away under guard. At last, on August 21 Klusmann and his lone comrade stumbled into the hands of friendly Meo guerrillas near Bouam Long. The brave pilot was one of only two naval aviators to escape from captivity during the entire Vietnam War.

On June 7, the day after Klusmann's loss, another RF-8A photo recce aircraft, now escorted by four F-8D Crusader fighters, returned to the Plain of Jars region. Again the enemy opened up with heavy anti-aircraft artillery (AAA) fire. One plane was hit. With orders to retaliate, the escorts attacked the defensive positions and then shepherded the flight back to Yankee Station.

Another mission did not go so well. Commander Doyle W. Lynn, skipper of *Kitty Hawk*'s Fighter Squadron 111, led two other F-8Ds and a reconnaissance plane back into central Laos. Over the target area Lynn's Crusader was riddled by ground fire, forcing the pilot to eject. He hit the ground uninjured in a forested area 35 miles south of Xieng Khouang.

This time, the SAR group was ready. Lynn's fellow pilots flew overhead cover until their fuel ran low. The carrier task group dispatched relief escorts and an A-3B communications relay plane. In addition, a flight of four Douglas A-1 Skyraiders, known as "Spads" arrived from their SAR alert position over Da Nang.

When the SAR force located the commander the next day, by guiding on the signal from his survival radio and then flares, they called in an H-34 Sea Horse helicopter. Thick overhead cover made the rescue tricky and dangerous, but the H-34 finally plucked Lynn from a small clearing. He returned to duty soon afterwards. As cruel fate would have it, Commander Lynn was shot down over North Vietnam the following year; this time he did not come out alive.

The loss of these aircraft led Washington leaders to up the ante in the psychological contest. Secretary of Defense McNamara instructed the JCS to order strikes against the antiaircraft sites at Xieng Khouang and Khang Khay. On June 9th, Air Force F-100 Super Sabres were despatched from Tan Son Nhut airfield, near Saigon, to bomb and rocket enemy positions at the first location.

But before Task Force 77 carried out its assigned attack on Khang Khay, set for the following day, Souvanna Phouma called a halt to all Yankee Team operations in Laos. He was vexed that the United

Cmdr. Doyle W. Lynn —rescued by helicopter after his Crusader was shot down over Laos.

FLYING EYES: An RF-8A Crusader and a larger RA-5C Vigilante (foreground) set off on a reconnaissance mission over North Vietnam. The RA-5C was fitted with omni-directional cameras capable of taking photographs in color, black-and-white, infrared and radar. In the early stages of the war photographic reconnaissance was of primary importance. US leaders wanted to learn the extent of communist infiltration along the Ho Chi Minh Trail of Laos and into South Vietnam.

States struck the Xieng Khouang site; he was even more distressed that details of American combat operations in Laos were reaching the public.

On June 14, once Souvanna was assured that information on this US military activity in Laos would not be disclosed in the future, the JCS restarted Yankee Team. In addition, to avoid further losses, McNamara insisted on a "minimum risk approach"; reconnaissance aircraft had to fly over 10,000 feet, above the range of most communist antiaircraft guns, unless American leaders needed low-level photographic coverage of a target. Washington

ordered air units to stay clear of "lead alley" and other areas crowded with antiaircraft weapons. During the rest of 1964, the Navy lost no aircraft over Laos and the Air Force only two. On the negative side, the quality of aerial photos diminished considerably. Further, these measures hardly increased the pressure on the North Vietnamese leaders in Hanoi.

In the new phase, which began for the Navy on June 19, *Constellation* dispatched four Crusader escorts, an RF-8A, and an RA-3B photo reconnaissance plane over the Laotian panhandle. The

Gen. William C. Westmoreland —commander of the US Military Assistance Command, Vietnam. In July 1964, Washington approved his request to shell North Veitnamese naval defenses.

heavy Skywarrior, affectionately known as the "Whale," was especially suited for aerial photography at the higher altitudes.

Ticonderoga took over Yankee Team duty on July 12 when the carrier and her escorts, under Rear Admiral Robert B. Moore, relieved *Constellation* at the mouth of Tonkin Gulf. *Constellation* rejoined *Ticonderoga* on August 5. Aircraft from these two hard-working flattops and from *Bon Homme Richard*, *Hancock*, and *Ranger* completed the year's photographic missions in Laos.

Ranger also introduced a new photo plane—the RA-5C Vigilante. This large, heavy aircraft, built to deliver nuclear bombs deep in enemy territory, gave the reconnaissance community a technologically advanced, high-flying platform. *Ranger* began operations with RA-5C "Viggies" on December 1

By the end of 1964 Task Force 77's Vigilante Crusader, and Skywarrior reconnaissance aircraft had conducted 171, or more than half, of the joint Yankee Team photographic missions. American commanders now received timely information on the number and size of North Vietnamese fighting units moving down the Ho Chi Minh Trail toward South Vietnam. For this reason, the operations were continued until the end of the war. They did not, however, influence the communists to give up their unification campaign.

US leaders turned to stronger measures. At the end of July, General William C. Westmoreland, the Commander US Military Assistance Command Vietnam, asked for authority to broaden the mission of the 34A force operating in North Vietnam. He wanted to use its maritime boat unit to shell radar sites, defense posts, and other coastal targets. The South Vietnamese-manned unit, which the US Naval Advisory Detachment, Da Nang, trained and equipped with eight Nasty-class fast patrol boats had irritated the communists that summer by seizing junks and sabotaging installations. Washington approved his request.

The first shore bombardment actions occurred on the night of July 30-31 against Hon Me and Hon Nieu, two islands in the Gulf of Tonkin.

In retaliation North Vietnamese PT boats attacked the destroyer *Maddox* cruising in the Gulf of Tonkin in the Desoto Patrol program. Heading

utheast on the afternoon of August 2, after patrol-
ing in international waters, *Maddox* was attacked
y three PT boats. The high-speed vessels
aunched at least four torpedoes and fired their 14.5
illimeter deck guns at the ship. The "fish" miss-
d, but one 14.5-millimeter round put a hole in the
estroyer's superstructure. But American gunners
it and slowed one of the motor torpedo boats.

Then four Crusaders screamed over *Maddox* at 400
nots and made for the enemy vessels, by now
eading away from the destroyer and miles north
f her. The jets were led by Commander—later Vice
dmiral and Medal of Honor winner—James B.
tockdale. He and his fellow F-8 pilots from
iconderoga were conducting practice firing runs
ear the ship when the radio call went out to fly to
he assistance of *Maddox*. They covered the 300
iles to the destroyer in one-half hour.

Once over the ship, the Crusader flight was guid-
d by the *Maddox* air controller, whose rapid-fire and
xcitable voice reminded Stockdale of Clem McCar-
hy, the well known 1930s radio boxing announcer.
Clem" relayed the orders of Captain John J. Her-
ick, the on-scene commander in *Maddox*, to attack
nd destroy the North Vietnamese vessels. Com-
ander Stockdale instructed experienced naval
viators Commander Robair Mohrhardt and Lieute-
ant Commander Ev Southwick of VF 53 to peel off

FLASHPOINT:
**The torpedo
attacks by
North
Vietnamese
patrol boats on
the destroyers
Maddox and
Turner Joy,
early in August
1964, marked
the surface
Navy's baptism
of fire in the
long Southeast
Asian conflict.
The attacks
brought swift
retaliation with
aircraft from
Constellation
and
Ticonderoga
bombing North
Vietnamese
naval units and
fuel facilities.**

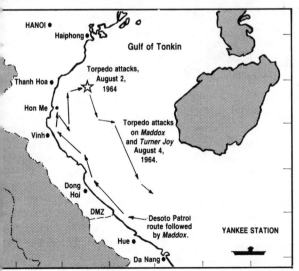

25

Cmdr. James B. Stockdale —led the retaliatory raid against the North Vietnamese PT boats that attacked *Maddox*. Later he was to be captured and held as a prisoner of war after his Crusader was downed by antiaircraft fire. On his release he was awarded the Medal of Honor. He was subsequently promoted to Vice Admiral.

and attack the damaged trailing boat while he and his squadron's new pilot, Lieutenant (j.g.) Dick Hastings, dropped on the two PTs in the lead. Stockdale passed through a spray of antiaircraft fire from one lead PT boat to fire off a Zuni rocket. It missed. Hastings, attacking the other boat, suddenly shouted over the radio that he was hit. Once the commander pulled alongside and saw that the damage was minor, he told the young pilot to orbit the destroyers and wait. Then the veteran naval aviator returned to the battle. Mohrhardt and Southwick were hard at work strafing all three boats

Turning Point

FIGHTER ARM: An F-8E Crusader, mainstay of the fleet's fighter arm in the early years of the war, in flight over South Vietnam. The single-seat, single-engine Crusader carried four air-to-air Sidewinder missiles and four 20mm cannon. The VF-53 painted beneath the "Navy" decal indicates that it was from *Ticonderoga*'s Fighter Squadron 53.

ith 20-millimeter cannon fire. They stopped one PT ead in the water, where it remained with smoke ouring from its spaces below. It later sank. tockdale made repeated passes over the boats, "hos-ng" them down with his four 20-millimeter guns. hen, with fuel reserves dwindling, the Crusader ilots broke off the action and headed for home. Iastings, however, was forced by the damage to his -8 to land at Da Nang Air Base.

For the next two days, August 3 and 4, *Maddox*, ow accompanied by destroyer *Turner Joy*, con-nued the patrol along the North Vietnamese coast.

27

The Johnson administration and its Pacific naval leaders were determined to reassert the traditional American support for freedom of the sea, the right to sail in international waters anywhere in the world.

Then, on the night of August 4th, the North Vietnamese struck again. About 70 miles off the coast communist naval vessels launched several torpedoes at *Turner Joy*. Fortunately, the torpedoes missed their mark. The two destroyers responded with heavy fire from their 5-inch and 3-inch guns, which sank or damaged several of the hostile craft.

Alerted to the approach of the enemy vessels, first by intelligence and then the ships' radars, Captain Herrick had called for air support. Within minutes *Ticonderoga* catapulted aircraft into the inky blackness. The first planes, armed, manned, and kept in readiness on deck, included two A-1H Skyraiders and one Crusader of the alert force. Following them were two A-4D Skyhawks and another four A-1Hs. A total of 16 aircraft from *Ticonderoga* and *Constellation*, the latter ship now steaming at flank speed from Hong Kong, supported the destroyers that night.

When the first aircraft arrived over *Maddox* and *Turner Joy*, they began circling the ships and swooping in on areas where Clem McCarthy reported enemy activity. The jets repeatedly opened up with their Zuni rockets and 20-millimeter guns. Commander Stockdale, pilot of the lone Crusader, stayed close to the water while the two Skyhawk aviators circled above. The night was overcast and pitch black and the destroyers' flares and star shell illumination devices, quickly swallowed up by clouds, gave off little light. Further, the jets flew too fast to loiter over a suspected target.

But other aviators did spot the furtive enemy. The commanding officer of VA 58, Commander George H. Edmondson, and his wingman, Lieutenant Jere A. Barton, flying the slower, prop-driven A-1H Skyraiders, made significant observations. Zooming ahead of both destroyers, Edmondson reported the snake-like wake of a high-speed vessel. Barton, on one of many evolutions around the battle area, spied a dark object, between the two destroyers, that soon moved off into the cloaking darkness. The pilots, both trained at finding surface vessels at night, also

Cmdr. Robert C. Barnhart —commander of the destroyer *Turner Joy* during the Gulf of Tonkin incident when it was attacked by two North Vietnamese PT boats. During the incident *Turner Joy* and the destroyer *Maddox* dropped depth charges and fired 249 shells before the enemy eventually broke contact.

ported seeing gun flashes and light bursts at their altitude, between 700 and 1,500 feet. They affirmed that an enemy vessel's antiaircraft fire was responsible.

By the early morning of August 5th, the action was over. Both destroyers were approaching the mouth of the gulf and dispatching reports about the North Vietnamese Navy's second attack on the US Seventh Fleet.

Much to the surprise of American leaders, civilian and military, rather than backing down in the face of US military pressure and curtailing their actions against South Vietnam, the North Vietnamese had resisted. Admiral Ulysses S. Grant Sharp, Jr., commander in chief of the US Pacific Command, called for retaliatory air strikes on the North Vietnamese Navy. Following the consultation with his National Security Council, President Johnson ordered a one-time reprisal strike, code-named Pierce Arrow, by carrier aircraft.

Constellation and Ticonderoga received the mission—to attack the North Vietnamese naval vessels based at Ben Thuy, Quang Khe, Hon Gay, and in the estuary to the Lach Chao River; and the fuel storage facility at Vinh.

Shortly after noon on August 5th, F-8 Crusaders, A-4 Skyhawks, and an RF-8A photo recce plane of Ticonderoga's Carrier Air Wing 5 catapulted off the angled deck and soon joined the ship's slower A-1H Skyraiders heading for the Vinh oil complex. Another flight of Crusaders and an RF-8A climbed into the sky and made for Quang Khe.

Constellation began launching her Carrier Air Wing 14 squadrons at 1300. The first planes airborne, propeller-driven A-1s groaning under the weight of bombs and rockets, split into two groups and struck out for Hon Gay and Lach Chao. At 1430 Skyhawk jets shot off Constellation's deck and raced to catch up with the slower Spads. F-4 Phantom IIs followed both strike groups to provide air cover. RF-8As went along to photograph bomb damage.

The iron hand of the Seventh Fleet's Attack Carrier Striking Force fell hard on North Vietnam. Commander Stockdale's Vinh strike force of Crusaders, Skyhawks, and Skyraiders, which first rendezvoused several miles offshore, crossed the

Adm. Ulysses S. Grant Sharp —Commander in Chief, Pacific, 1964-1968. He called for a strong US response to the North Vietnamese torpedo attacks on the destroyer *Maddox*. Later he would direct the Rolling Thunder bombing campaign against North Vietnam.

Cmdr Wesley L. McDonald —led the Skyhawk raid in the surprise attack against the Vinh fuel complex.

coast near Ha Tinh and raced for the target. Commander Stockdale and his flight leaders chose this route because a group of hills to the south of Vinh masked approaching aircraft from radar and antiaircraft guns until the last moment.

The strike group pressed on. As planned, the bomb-laden A-1Hs climbed over the hills to gain dive-bombing altitude, while Commander Wesley L. McDonald's VA 56 Skyhawks raced up a valley below them. The Crusaders skimmed over the sea along the coast, passed the river entrance to Vinh and then turned back south.

Still no alarm was raised as *Ticonderoga*'s combat formation converged on the fuel complex—14 large storage tanks neatly aligned in a fenced enclosure.

At 1330 the Crusaders screamed down from 15,000 feet over the red-tiled roofs of the city and loosed fury of rocket and 20-millimeter fire against silent antiaircraft positions. Simultaneously, the A-4 "Scooters" emerged from the north end of the valley through the hills and fell on other guns.

Seconds later, the lumbering Spads of VA 52 crested the rise and dove down in column to join two Skyhawks for the attack on the fuel tanks. They dropped 28,000 pounds of general purpose bombs and fired Zuni rockets right on target. The enclosure erupted in fire and smoke that rose thousands of feet in the air. The attack was over in minutes.

The group then zipped over to the nearby Ben Thuy naval base where they sank one armed vessel and damaged three others. That afternoon, eight "Tico" A-4s returned and destroyed the remaining fuel tanks at Vinh and sank two more naval vessels at Ben Thuy. The surprise operation was a complete success.

At Quang Khe to the south, the F-8s of VF 53 also achieved surprise. The Crusaders caught enemy vessels at anchor or trying to escape from the harbor to the open sea. They riddled five boats and sank another with cannon and rocket fire.

At Hon Gay, *Constellation*'s VA 144 Skyhawks streaked in from the southeast at 1540 and opened up on Swatow gunboats and other craft, sending them scattering about the harbor to avoid the American fire. Antiaircraft weapons on the vessels and ashore returned fire, filling the air with

Turning Point

ELEVATOR RIDE:

A-4 Skyhawks wait their turn on the elevator at hangar level on the *Constellation*. Nicknamed the "Scooter" by its pilots for the way it scooted like a balsa plane off the steam catapult, the A-4 flew more bombing missions in the Vietnam War than any other aircraft. With its delta wings only 27 feet 6 inches from tip-to-tip, the single-seat bomber was so compact that it did not require folding wings for storage aboard ship.

Turning Point

FIRST LINE OF DEFENSE: North Vietnamese Navy gunners man the forward 37mm antiaircraft weapon of a Swatow motor gunboat as another Swatow leads the way through waters off the coast of North Vietnam. These 83-foot vessels were the enemy's first-line combatants in a fleet that consisted of 24 Swatows, 12 P-4 PT boats, and 50 other craft.

crisscrossing tracer rounds and acrid black shell bursts.

When Lieutenant (j.g.) Everett Alvarez came around for another pass, enemy fire struck and disabled his A-4. The pilot quickly ejected from his doomed aircraft and landed safely on shore. His comrades called in an Air Force HU-16 amphibian aircraft standing by on SAR alert. Unfortunately, enemy troops were seen closing in on Alvarez and the terrain was too rugged to try a rescue. The on-scene commander recalled the HU-16. The young pilot was the first naval aviator captured in North Vietnam. Showing remarkable bravery and endurance, Alvarez withstood the cruel treatment of his captors until release in 1973.

As the downed pilot's comrades continued to pepper the enemy guns, VA 145's Skyraiders roared in to attack the coastal fleet. When they banked and headed out to sea, they left behind two burning Swatows and a motor torpedo boat and three damaged or sunk vessels.

On their way to the Lach Chao Estuary, the Carrier Air Wing 14 aircraft passed near Hon Ne Island. Just then, one of the pilots spotted five enemy naval vessels below. Five Skyhawk jets zeroed in on three boats to the north while four Spads pounced on the two to the south.

Enemy antiaircraft gunners opened up, hitting Lieutenant James S. Hardie's Skyraider. Disregarding the damage, Hardie continued his attack run and then flew his shot-up plane back to "Connie" for a successful emergency landing.

Another pilot was not so lucky. On his third run at the fire-spitting vessels, Lieutenant (j.g.) Richard C. Sather's Skyraider was knocked down. He was the first naval aviator killed in the Vietnam War, but the Vietnamese did not return his body to the United States until 1985. Sather and Hardie did not go unavenged, for their comrades heavily damaged all five enemy craft, leaving several dead in the water.

Aerial photographs and visual reports revealed that all but three of the 36 PT boats or Swatow gunboats in the North Vietnamese Navy were hit in the Pierce Arrow strike. The Americans sank seven vessels and severely damaged another ten for the loss of two pilots. Of the 67 carrier aircraft taking part, two were damaged and two destroyed.

Lt. James S. Hardie —managed to skilfully nurse his shot-up A-1 Skyraider back to *Constellation*. The naval aviator from Carrier Air Wing 14 had taken part in the Pierce Arrow retaliatory strikes against the North Vietnamese Navy in August 1964, when his plane was hit by antiaircraft fire. Undeterred, he went on to complete his bomb run before making for home.

Turning Point

MAN-IN-THE-MIDDLE: An air officer and his assistant supervising preparations for launching aircraft from the carrier *Bon Homme Richard*. Located in Primary Flight Control, the glassed-in control tower jutting over the flight deck, a carrier's air officer was responsible for the smooth-running of the flight deck. The pressure was greatest after combat missions when returning planes were low on fuel. Assessing priorities correctly determined whether everyone landed safely aboard or in the drink.

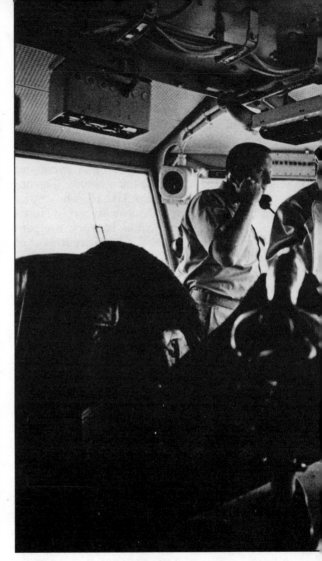

If the destructive Pierce Arrow attack impressed the North Vietnamese with America's determination to have its way in Southeast Asia, that impression soon faded. Fearful of provoking Chinese intervention, the Johnson administration eased the military pressure on North Vietnam during the remaining months of 1964. After the conclusion of the August Desoto Patrol, US destroyers did not repeat a surveillance operation along the North Vietnamese coast until mid-September. Following that cruise, by *Morton* and *Richard S. Edwards*, the

COME IN: Down on the deck a landing signal officer advises a Phantom II as it passes over the stern of a carrier at 135 mph. The arresting hook is visible below the rear of the jet. After touchdown the hook snags the arresting cable, bringing the plane to a halt.

Desoto Patrol was ended. American leaders also suspended the covert 34A maritime operation until October. The rough seas and rain squalls of the winter monsoon, combined with tight control of operations from Washington, limited the number of attacks by South Vietnamese coastal raiders during the rest of the year. The carrier presence in the Gulf of Tonkin also diminished. After the third week in September, usually only one attack carrier steamed at Yankee Station.

US reluctance to take stronger actions against

President Lyndon B. Johnson —ruled out retaliation bombing after Viet Cong attacks on US installation in late 1964. Instead he sanctioned Barrel Roll—the codename for a campaign of armed reconnaissance missions over Laos.

North Vietnam persisted even when the communists attacked US military installations and servicemen in South Vietnam. After the Viet Cong mortared Bien Hoa Air Base outside of Saigon on November 1, wrecking 24 aircraft and killing or wounding 76 Americans, President Johnson vetoed reprisal strikes by Task Force 77 and Air Force aircraft against the North. Again, on Christmas Eve, the communists blew up the Brink Bachelor Officers Quarters in downtown Saigon, killing two Americans and wounding over 100 Americans, Vietnamese, and Australians. The president ruled out retaliation bombing for fear of provoking further communist attacks or escalating the conflict.

Instead, Washington leaders decided to turn up the heat on North Vietnam in another arena—Laos. On December 12 President Johnson approved the start of armed reconnaissance in eastern Laos by US aircraft. This meant a search by combat planes for enemy trucks, personnel, bridges, and supply dumps along infiltration routes leading to South Vietnam and central Laos. When the American air units discovered enemy targets, they were authorized to attack.

On December 17, three days after the US Air Force inaugurated this campaign, code-named Barrel Roll, A-1Hs and F-4Bs of *Ranger*'s Carrier Air Wing 9 bombed and strafed a logistic staging facility and a bridge in the Laotian panhandle. The aircraft destroyed storage buildings, but missed the bridge. Air Force F-105 Thunderchiefs from Tan Son Nhut air base flew the next two road surveillance missions, with limited results. Then, on the 30th, Skyraiders from newly arrived *Hancock* bombed and destroyed six buildings. Three days later, A-4E Skyhawks, flown for the first time in Laos, flattened another three buildings. On January 10, 1965, *Hancock* A-1Hs strafed three motorcycles and an ox-cart on Laotian Route 23 and then demolished seven buildings. American leaders soon recognized that these pinpricks had little effect. North Vietnamese operations on the Ho Chi Minh Trail continued without letup.

The first meaningful strike of Barrel Roll occurred on the 13th when Air Force planes destroyed the Ban Ken Bridge cutting a main road link between North Vietnam and the Plain of Jars. Communist truck traffic backed up east of the collapsed span, but these inviting targets were off limits under existing operational restrictions; strikes had to be at least 48 hours apart.

If nothing else, the Barrel Roll and Yankee Team operations forced the communists to run truck convoys at night. To also deny them the cloak of darkness, Task Force 77 began nighttime air patrols. On January 15, A-1H Skyraiders flew the first such Barrel Roll mission and scoured Route 23 in the panhandle for trucks. It was not an auspicious beginning. The Spads soon located a five-vehicle convoy and shot it up. However, the flight leader then lost his bearings in the dark. Believing themselves correctly oriented, two pilots bombed a village that appeared to contain communist supply vehicles— unfortunately, Laotian government troops garrisoned the village. The damage and casualties were minor but Souvanna Phouma was incensed. He ordered a halt to the entire Barrel Roll operation. He relented after eight days, when assured that the accident was a freak, but the incident was one more indication that the American campaign to pressure the North Vietnamese into line was in trouble.

The enemy, far from cowed, continued the campaign of intimidation. On February 7, 1965, the Viet Cong killed eight Americans and wounded 109 others when they mortared the US advisors' compound at Pleiku in the Central Highlands of South Vietnam.

As planned at the end of 1964, the Johnson administration was ready to one-up the communists in this contest of wills. The president ordered a one-time-only, "tit-for-tat" reprisal air strike by US Navy, US Air Force, and South Vietnamese squadrons against military barracks in the Democratic Republic of Vietnam. The operation was designated Flaming Dart I.

That same day *Ranger*, *Hancock*, and *Coral Sea* dispatched aircraft for strikes on the barracks at Vit Thu Lu and Dong Hoi, both just north of the Demilitarized Zone between North and South Vietnam. *Ranger*'s attack on Vit Thu Lu was soon scrubbed because of heavy clouds over the target. The weather was little better at Dong Hoi, but the massed air units of the other two carriers bore in on the compound, home of the 325th Infantry Division.

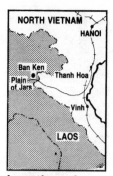

Location of Ban Ken Bridge —the first target of Barrel Roll

Flight time — Lt. (j.g.) Charles E. Frederick checks the status board aboard *Bonne Homme Richard* to discover the time and mission he will be flying over Vietnam.

Leading the attack were *Coral Sea*'s 29 aircraft of Carrier Air Wing 15, which crossed the coastline south of Dong Hoi, headed north, and approached the target under a low cloud ceiling. Screaming in at 500 knots, they hit the barracks with rockets and 250-pound bombs.

The North Vietnamese gunners were ready, meeting *Coral Sea*'s aviators with a curtain of lead from 37-millimeter guns, automatic weapons, and small arms. The Swatow gunboats in the Kien River

THE DAY OF THE SPAD:

Lt. (j.g.) Frederick's Douglas A-1H Skyraider being launched from the *Bonne Homme Richard*. Known as the "Spad," the veteran multipurpose bomber was the last piston-engined attack airplane to be flown from a US aircraft carrier. First flown in 1944, the Spad was eventually withdrawn from operations over North Vietnam in 1968 by the Navy—but not before the propeller-driven plane had notched up considerable achievements, including downing two enemy MiG-17 jets.

added their firepower to the barrage. Before the attack squadrons, VA 153 and VA 155, completed their bombing dives and headed out to sea, antiaircraft fire struck Lieutenant Edward A. Dickson's A-4 Skyhawk. The brave pilot finished his attack and then bailed out of the flaming aircraft. Tragically, his parachute failed to open and Dickson plummeted to his death.

No sooner had the first echelon cleared the target than *Hancock*'s Carrier Air Wing 21 units joined the

fray. Seventeen Skyhawks from VA 212 and VA 216 rolled in, strafing and bombing camp facilities. Simultaneously, F-8 Crusaders attacked antiaircraft positions. Right behind the leading units came RF-8A reconnaissance aircraft to photograph the results.

Naval leaders were not impressed. Of 275 buildings in the camp, only 16 were destroyed and another six damaged. The heavy cloud cover and low ceiling had made it difficult to attack from the proper bombing angle.

The reprisal did little to restrain the communists. Three days later they blew up the American barracks at Qui Nhon in South Vietnam, inflicting 44 casualties.

Again, Washington ordered a limited retaliatory air action. On February 11, *Ranger* launched her Skyraiders as the first element in the one-day multi-aircraft operation, code-named Flaming Dart II. Ninety-nine planes from *Ranger*, *Hancock*, and *Coral Sea* were dispatched against the enemy barracks at Chanh Hoa while US Air Force and South Vietnamese Air Force units were assigned to strike at enemy targets in the Vu Con cantonment in North Vietnam.

At 1400 *Ranger* Skyraiders and Skyhawks descended on Chanh Hoa, dropping 1,000 and 250-pound bombs and firing rockets into the camp. The massed squadrons from *Hancock* and *Coral Sea* followed up the first wave and added their firepower.

Meanwhile, F-8E Crusaders and F-4B Phantoms rocketed and strafed the numerous AAA sites around Chanh Hoa. The entire operation was directed by Commander Warren H. Sells, the commanding officer of *Hancock*'s Carrier Air Wing 21, who loitered over the battle in a command-communications plane. Another 33 Crusaders, Phantoms, and Skyraiders flew overhead cover in case the communists sent in any of the 53 MiG interceptors based near Hanoi. They did not for now. Despite the lack of MiG opposition, the enemy defenders hit hard. One *Coral Sea* A-4C, shot-up by flak, limped south to Da Nang. The pilot landed his Skyhawk safely but unused bombs slung underneath the wings exploded, destroying the aircraft. Lieutenant William T. Majors of VA 153 also escaped death when he bailed out of his stricken plane over the gulf. The SAR group responded immediately and an Air Force HU-16 plucked Majors out of the water and whisked him away to Da Nang.

Lieutenant Commander Robert H. Shumaker of Fighter Squadron 154 was not so fortunate. While attacking a gun position at Chanh Hoa, his Crusader was hit. It spun out of control. Unable to reach the relative safety of the sea, Shumaker ejected in North Vietnam. He was immediately captured and imprisoned with Lieutenant Alvarez.

The air strike on Chanh Hoa was a moderate success, with the destruction or damage of one-third of the cantonment's 76 buildings. Still, US leaders harbored few illusions that the reprisal would persuade the North Vietnamese to abandon their goals in South Vietnam and Laos.

After more than a year, the campaign of graduated pressure against the North had failed. Despite the

Fire and reconnaissance —Twenty millimeter cannon fire from an A-4 Skyhawk boils the waters of a North Vietnamese river as the aircraft carries out an attack on barges carrying military goods. The Skyhawk, part of VA 55 from *Ranger*, carried an automatic camera in a pod below its fuselage to record the results.

Turning Point

ON TAPE: On board the *Midway* a logboard records the exact time and date as an A-4 Skyhawk catches the No. 1 wire to land safely.
Video recordings of aircraft launch and recovery were an invaluable aid to increasing safety and decreasing error. With the use of tapes made on PLAT (Pilot Landing Aid, TV) pilots, air officers and flight deck crews could evaluate individual launches and landings to check for equipment malfunction and improve flight deck procedures.

continuous show-of-force carrier deployments off the mainland, 34A coastal raiding operation, Yankee Team photographic reconnaissance program, Barrel Roll armed reconnaissance, and Pierce Arrow and Flaming Dart reprisal strikes, the North Viet-

amese were not intimidated—quite the opposite.
The attacks on American personnel and installa-
ions in South Vietnam and the naval sorties against
Maddox and *Turner Joy* revealed a foe with lots of
ght left in him.

Rolling Thunder

2

Attacks on Hanoi and Haiphong

HE Johnson administration ordered the strongest measure yet—the sustained bombing of North Vietnam. American leaders intended to bomb military targets in the south and then systematically work north toward the industrial and warmaking heart around Hanoi and Haiphong. The pressure would not ease until Ho Chi Minh called off his offensive in South Vietnam and Laos.

While President Johnson and his chief advisors hoped this strategy would achieve the long-sought objective, by early 1965 they were not overly optimistic. So, Washington also began deploying US ground, air, and naval forces to help defend South Vietnam against assault from within and without.

On March 8, the Seventh Fleet Amphibious Task Force (Task Force 76) landed elements of the 9th Marine Expeditionary Brigade at Da Nang. *Hancock* units flew air cover. The Marines were the vanguard of a force that reached over half a million men in 1968. On the 11th, the fleet began combined operations with the Vietnamese Navy to patrol the 1,200-mile coast of South Vietnam against seaborne infiltrators.

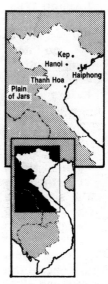

Meanwhile the bombing campaign, code-named Rolling Thunder, sputtered to a start. Originally scheduled for February 20, the first strike was not launched for two weeks because of another coup attempt in Saigon, poor flying weather over the north, and international political complications. This was a harbinger of things to come. Finally, on March 2, the US and South Vietnamese air forces struck Xom Bang and Quang Khe while *Ranger* and *Coral Sea* aircraft began tactical aerial reconnaissance over North Vietnam, called Blue Tree.

Carrier forces launched Rolling Thunder on

45

Rolling Thunder

LAUNCH!: A catapult officer signals "launch" seconds before a *Coral Sea* Skyhawk attack jet screams down the flight deck in late March 1965. Once airborne the A-4 would go into a holding pattern over the carrier before joining other aircraft in a multi-squadron, or "Alpha", strike against North Vietnamese radar sites. The wisps of steam escaping from the catapult track came from one of the carrier's eight boilers. These provided the enormous belch of steam necessary to catapult a Skyhawk from zero to 170 knots in a few hundred feet.

March 15, when 64 Skyhawks and Skyraiders from *Hancock* and *Ranger* pounded the Phu Qui ammunition depot with 250-pound bombs, rockets, and cannon fire, and for the first time in the North, napalm bombs. They destroyed or damaged numerous buildings. A restrike by Air Force planes shortly afterward added to the destruction.

All but one of the 94 attack, flak suppression, escort, and photo recce planes in this multi-squadron "Alpha strike" returned to the carriers. Lieutenant (j.g.) Charles F. Clydesdale went down with his Spad when he was forced to ditch it in the gulf.

As Rolling Thunder got into full swing during the spring, the Navy and Air Force sought to accomplish political objective: to force the enemy to negotiate peace settlement; and several military objectives: to diminish or stop the flow of personnel and unit reinforcements, munitions, and supplies to South Vietnam; to destroy the facilities in North Vietnam that supported the war; and to cut off Hanoi from outside support.

These political and military goals proved impossible to achieve as the North Vietnamese put up stout resistance and Washington severely restricted the US military's operational freedom. Pilots were not allowed to fly within 30 nautical miles of the border with communist China, for fear of provoking Chinese intervention. In order not to hit foreign embassies or kill government leaders with which the administration hoped to negotiate a solution to the war, US forces were prohibited from attacking targets within ten nautical miles of the center of Hanoi. A zone four nautical miles from the heart of Haiphong, the chief port, was made offlimits to avoid US aircraft bombing the Soviet, Chinese, and other communist and non-communist merchant ships. Further, within a 30-mile radius of Hanoi and a 10-mile radius of Haiphong, American air units could not strike communist AAA and surface-to-air missile (SAM) sites unless the enemy fired first.

Of course, the North Vietnamese used these sanctuaries to stockpile mountains of weapons, ammunition, military supplies, and essential raw materials. They also became the centers of the air defense system that featured air bases filled to capacity with Soviet-built MiG aircraft; surface-to-air missile installations bristling with weapons; antiaircraft parks with guns of all sizes and ranges; and command-communications facilities to control them

AERIAL DEFENSE: A *Yorktown* ordnanceman arms an A-4C Skyhawk with a Sidewinder air-to-air missile. During this deployment to Southeast Asia, in early 1965, the carrier's attack squadrons flew combat missions against Laotian and North Vietnamese forces on the Ho Chi Minh Trail. The heat-seeking Sidewinders were carried by American aircraft in case communist MiGs attacked the carrier air units. They did not—for now.

ll. In addition, this allowed the enemy to beef up his defenses around those targets he knew the Americans were limited to.

In spite of these hindrances, the Seventh Fleet had formidable forces. Two or three aircraft carriers formed the core of Task Force 77 during 1965. The large-deck Forrestal-class ships operated up to 100 aircraft while the smaller carriers accommodated 70 to 80. Generally two fighter and three attack squadrons and other specialized aircraft detachments made up a carrier air wing. The well-liked F-8 Crusader flew fighter escort and flak suppression missions while the versatile F-4 Phantom II served as a fighter and an attack plane. Initially, the main-line attack aircraft were the old reliable, piston-engine A-1 Skyraider and the quick A-4 Skyhawk jet. RF-8A Crusaders and RA-3B Skywarriors, and the technologically sophisticated RA-5C Vigilantes carried out the unglamorous and dangerous photo reconnaissance missions. Specially converted Skyraiders and Skywarriors used electronic countermeasures (ECM) equipment to confound enemy radar and communications. Known as E-1B Tracers, their electronic gear served to warn of approaching MiGs, guide other American aircraft, and relay communications. Another Skywarrior version, the KA-3B, operated as an aerial refueler. The "Whale" carried over 5,000 gallons of jet fuel. Rounding out the carrier air wing were the large SH-3 Sea King and UH-2 Seasprite helicopters for search and rescue work.

The Task Force 77 squadrons carried a lethal arsenal of bombs, rockets, missiles, and other ordnance, including 250-, 500-, 750-, 1,000- and 2,000-pound general-purpose bombs and napalm bombs; 5-inch Zuni and 2.75-inch rockets; Bullpup air-to-surface weapons; Sidewinder and Sparrow air-to-air and Shrike anti-radar missiles; and 20-millimeter guns.

The attack carrier, despite its awesome weapons and aircraft, would have been useless if not for the unceasing efforts of the crew to ready the ship for combat. Working on a 24-hour schedule, the crew of 4,000 men maintained the powerful propulsion systems far below deck, issued supplies and commissary items, and served chow to an army of hungry sailors. Doctors, dentists, and hospital corps

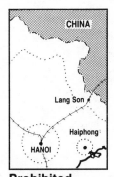

Prohibited zones —Political considerations dictated where and when American flyers could attack. When the delayed Rolling Thunder campaign began in March 1965, targets within a 30-mile radius of Hanoi and a 10-mile radius of Haiphong were declared off limits. Pilots were also prohibited from flying within 30 nautical miles of the border with China.

men cared for their physical and emotional needs.

In other spaces, naval officers and men poured over the latest intelligence on enemy targets and air defenses and prepared pre-flight briefings. In the hangar deck, just below the flight deck, plane captains and mechanics spent long hours making sure their sophisticated and delicate "birds" were ready to fly. The demands on planes and personnel were considerable. They had to be able to withstand catapulting off the deck at 200 knots, high "G" maneuvering in the hostile North Vietnamese sky, and the bone-jarring touch down and arrested landing.

In the "island," that part of a carrier jutting above the flight deck, other men plotted aircraft deck posi-

ions, navigated the mighty vessel, and monitored radar and communications systems. The carrier division commander and the ship's CO oversaw all of his work from their perches on the bridge.

Most of the time, their eyes were on the flight deck – an aircraft carrier's noisy and dangerous center of activity. During a launch, hundreds of busy men moved about the deck: red-shirted ordnancemen loaded bombs, rockets, missiles, and gun ammunition onto aircraft while fire fighters stood by with extinguishers and hoses; blue-shirted plane handlers prepared to disengage chocks and chains from tethered aircraft; plane captains, in their brown shirts, helped aviators get strapped in and made last-minute inspections; green-shirted catapult operators

GROUND SUPPORT:
The F-8 Crusader was heavily used in Rolling Thunder. Here an F-8 fires off a rocket during a ground support operation in South Vietnam.

Secretary of Defense Robert S. McNamara —gave guidance on the targets for Rolling Thunder.

built up pressure in their steam-powered systems and the flight deck directors, in yellow shirts, guided the jets with their screaming engines onto the catapult tracks. When all was ready these men gave the signal and the aircraft shot out of a steam cloud and into the blue.

Powerful as they were, the attack carriers could not have mounted a continuous air offensive in Southeast Asia without the support of other Seventh Fleet forces. Cruisers and destroyers shielded the flattops against enemy aircraft, ships, and submarines and worked with SAR aircraft to rescue downed fliers. The Mobile Logistic Support Force (Task Force 73), with its oilers, tenders, ammunition stores, repair, and salvage ships kept Task Force 77 on Yankee Station well supplied with "beans, bullets, and black oil." The tried-and-true method of underway replenishment, where logistic vessels steamed alongside carriers to deliver supplies, was improved by the use of ship-to-ship helicopter transfers, or "vertical replenishment."

In theory, the Navy's air operations in Southeast Asia were controlled by the Pacific Fleet commander through his subordinate Seventh Fleet commander who in turn directed the activity of Commander Task Force 77. However, throughout the war specific guidance on attack units, weapons, targets, and other details of planned air strikes came directly from the White House or the Secretary of Defense's office. The JCS and CINCPAC sometimes served only to pass on this information to the operational commanders.

At the tactical level, however, control of operations evolved in light of the combat experience. The first year of war, 1965, witnessed significant changes in the way the Navy and the Air Force handled the air campaign. As they worked their way up the North Vietnamese panhandle, each service hit targets on an alternating basis, every three hours. This was cumbersome. Then in November, each service alternated strikes on a weekly basis in six permanent geographic zones, or route packages. By the end of the year the American air forces had ironed out many of the previous command and control difficulties.

Resolution of this issue, however, was still in the future when *Coral Sea* and *Hancock* air units

tepped up Rolling Thunder operations in the spring
f 1965. From March 26 to 31, the two carriers' air
vings carried out "radar bursting" strikes against
acilities the enemy relied on to pinpoint American
ircraft over the gulf. On the first day, 70 planes hit
adar sites on Cape Ron, at Vinh Son, and Ha Tinh,
nd on Bach Long Vi or Nightingale Island.

This last site was strategically located in the mid-
le of the gulf between North Vietnam and China's
Iainan Island. The attack on the 26th failed to
estroy the island's radar, so three days later
nother 70 aircraft concentrated on this one target.
s *Coral Sea*'s attack squadrons dove on the target
hrough a 5,000-foot cloud ceiling, they were met by
storm of fire thrown up by the antiaircraft guns
rowded onto the small island.

Almost at once, enemy gunners hit the aircraft of
hree squadron commanders leading their units in-
o battle.

Commander Jack Harris, CO of VA 155, bailed out
f his stricken attack plane and parachuted into the
ea. To his great surprise, a US submarine, serving
s "plane guard" for downed aircraft, surfaced near-
y and took him safely on board. VA 153's skipper,
'ommander Pete Mongilardi, used his long ex-
erience and skill to bring his shot-up A-4 Skyhawk
ack to *Coral Sea*. With fuel streaming from a port
ide tank, Mongilardi radioed for an A-3 tanker air-
raft to meet him en route to the carrier. Once the
wo planes rendezvoused, they proceeded in tandem,
vith fuel pumped from the "Whale" through a con-
ecting hose into Mongilardi's leaking Skyhawk. In
his way, the resourceful commander made it home
o his ship.

The third CO, Commander William N. Donnelly
f Fighter Squadron 154, survived to tell a harrow-
ng tale. As he led his flight into a high-speed dive,
is F-8 Crusader, hit earlier in the battle, spun out
f control and plunged toward the sea. Only
noments before impact, the pilot punched out of his
pside-down aircraft. After a violent low-level ejec-
ion, his body knifed into the water. Donnelly was
everely injured. He had cracked six vertebrae and
islocated his left shoulder. Although able to inflate
is life raft, it took him hours to climb on board the
ubber raft.

Like fellow naval aviator Ensign George Gay at

Cdr. Jack R.
Harris
—saved by a
submarine after
he bailed out
of his aircraft
and parachuted
into the sea.

SHARK SURVIVOR: Cdr. William N. Donnelly, of VF-154, returning to a welcome on board *Coral Sea* after spending 45 hours in the shark-infested waters of the Gulf of Tonkin. His F-8 Crusader was hit by antiaircraft fire during an attack on the radar station on the island of Bach Long Vi.

the Battle of Midway in World War II, Donnelly splashed only a few miles north of the day's fight. The American air strike had smashed the radar facility and touched off an ammunition dump which burned furiously. The pilot witnessed it all from his watery vantage point.

All night long a Chinese destroyer played its searchlight around the commander's position and cruised in search of him. Lady luck was with him. Finally, after enduring 45 hours in the water, he was spotted by *Hancock* planes which called in an Air Force HU-16 amphibian from the SAR group. When the aircraft splashed down, a paramedic jumped in to the water. He pulled the injured and weakened aviator on board—just before a circling school of sharks closed in.

Following a final strike against radar on Cape Ron on March 31, Task Force 77 began a month-long campaign to sever enemy lines of communication (LOC) below the 20th parallel. The objective was to reduce the flow of men and supplies feeding the war in South Vietnam and to isolate the southern battlefield from logistic support.

US Navy and Air Force units targeted key bridges, ferries, and points along railways and roads where the geography helped the attackers. These latter areas, called "choke points," were the hardest places for the North Vietnamese to bypass. American aircraft flew armed reconnaissance along the critical railways and roads in the panhandle in search of supply trains, trucks in convoy or alone, and repair parties.

The LOC campaign jumped off on April 3, when Commander Warren Sells's Carrier Air Wing 21 off *Hancock* and Commander H. P. Glindeman's Carrier Air Wing 15 off *Coral Sea* struck the Dong Phuong Thong Bridge 70 miles south of Hanoi on Route 1. The squadrons dropped 60 tons of ordnance on the structure during the morning and afternoon—cratering the approaches and knocking down the center span.

That day North Vietnamese MiGs entered the war. An F-8 fighter flying over Dong Phuong Thong was set upon by three MiG-15s which riddled the Crusader and raced out of danger. The American plane limped home.

The next day four MiG-17s broke through the clouds over Thanh Hoa and knocked two Air Force F-105 Thunderchiefs out of the sky. These had been attacking the key Ham Rong Bridge over the Ma River.

Even more ominous, two days later a *Coral Sea* photo recce plane flying a Blue Tree reconnaissance mission 15 miles southeast of Hanoi brought back evidence that the enemy was constructing a surface-to-air missile position. The Task Force 77 commander, Rear Admiral Edward C. Outlaw, alerted his superiors and recommended an attack to obliterate the site before the missiles were ready to fire. President Johnson vetoed the plan! He feared killing Soviet technicians reportedly helping to set up the weapons.

On May 12 the Johnson administration halted bombing of the North to see if the enemy was chastened enough to negotiate a compromise; he was not. North Vietnam returned a diplomatic note from the United States unopened.

Thus rebuffed, the Americans resumed Rolling Thunder with a vengeance. On May 18 more than 100 carrier aircraft pounced on the unsuspecting

Operational instructions —Cdr. Warren Sells, Commander of Carrier Air Wing 21, briefing pilots aboard *Hancock* for a mission over North Vietnam. On April 3, 1965 Sells and Cdr H. P. Glindeman of Carrier Air Wing 15 led the bombing campaign to sever enemy rail and road links. The opening strike against a vital bridge 70 miles south of Hanoi brought instant response with enemy MiG jets engaging US aircraft in air-to-air combat for the first time.

Rolling Thunder

MISSION ACCOMPLISHED: Smoke pours from a ruined North Vietnamese supply depot after it was attacked by 70 planes from the *Midway* on April 30, 1965. Forty tons of bombs were dropped on the military depot with devastating accuracy, leaving the surrounding homes and farmlands undamaged. This photo was taken by a photo-reconnaissance aircraft from *Midway* after clouds of black smoke, which had osbcured the target for much of the attack, had disappeared.

enemy at Phu Qui, wiping out 90 percent of the fu[...]
storage facility.

Attack units also flew night armed reco[...]
naissance. Commander Harry Thomas, CO of *Co[...]
al Sea*'s VA 153, adopted an effective tactic for spo[...]
ting trucks that he learned during the Korean Wa[...]
Normally, two A-4 Skyhawks, one orbiting 1,00[...]
feet above the other, circled bridges, ferry crossing[...]
and critical road segments. When the lower pil[...]
discovered an enemy vehicle he called for flares an[...]

Rolling Thunder

ADDED PUNCH: This formerly-classified photo shows a developmental model of the two-seat Intruder attack plane surrounded by all the bombs, rockets, missiles, and other ordnance it was equipped to deliver. This all-weather, day-night aircraft, capable of carrying a maximum bombload of 15,000 pounds, added real punch to the fleet's air arm when it was introduced in July 1965.

en dove on the exposed target. Although Commander Thomas was killed over North Vietnam that ear, his ingenious tactic lived on.

Naval leaders recognized, however, that despite ich innovations the war would not be over in weeks nd that the ever-increasing air operations in North ietnam, South Vietnam, and Laos would wear out ie men and machines of the four carriers deployed i the Western Pacific. As a result, early in June ie Navy added one more attack carrier to the

First kills —Cmdr. Louis C. Page and Lt. Cmdr. John C. Smith, scored one of the first aerial victories of the war when their Phantom downed a MiG-17 with a Sparrow missile on June 17, 1965. In the same action Page's wingman, Lt. (j.g.) David Batson and his back-seat radio intercept officer (RIO) Lt. Cmdr. Robert B. Doremus, downed the other MiG-17.

powerful Seventh Fleet, transferring the *I dependence* from the Atlantic Fleet.

Aside from the usual complement of aircraft, "*I dy*" steamed into the war zone with a squadron the new Grumman A-6A Intruder attack planes. Th Intruder was the best all-around naval attac bomber of the Vietnam War. Its advanced electron navigational and weapon delivery systems enable the plane to fly day or night and in all weather— blessing in Southeast Asia, where the communis skillfully used darkness and foul weather to figh and survive. The "pug-nosed," twin-engine Intrude operated by a pilot and bombardier/navigator (B/N seated side by side, could also fly long distances. Fu ther, the jet was able to carry 15,000 pounds of or nance; this surpassed the load capacity of the B-2 strategic bomber of World War II fame.

As the *Independence* A-6A squadron, the VA 7 "Sunday Punchers", prepared for combat, siste units continued striking supply lines. Aircraft fro *Midway* hit the soon-to-be famous Ham Rong bridg over the Ma River at Thanh Hoa for the first tim on June 17, 1965. The Ham Rong, or "Dragon Jaw", Bridge carried rail and road traffic south i to the panhandle. Aside from its strategic value, th bridge was the pride and joy of the Ho Chi Min regime, which invested great resources and prestig in its construction. Loss of the "Dragon's Jaw would be a devastating blow to the enemy war effor

Try as they might over the next three year neither the Navy nor the Air Force could drop th structure into the river. The bridge was 540 feet lor and 56 feet wide. Its two steel spans were anchore in the middle of the river on a gigantic concrete pie and on equally strong abutments on both bank Further, the structure was reinforced throughou the war.

Whenever naval aviators penetrated the defensiv fire thrown up by the many antiaircraft guns an guided their Bullpup missiles, 500-, 750-, 1,000-, an 2,000-pound bombs into the long, thin structure, th ordnance often caused only superficial damage.

In contrast to the experience of *Midway*'s attac pilots, the June 17 operation over Thanh Hoa wa an auspicious occasion for the carrier's "fighte jocks". Flying air cover, in the Navy's standard tw aircraft "Loose Deuce" tactical formation, Com

ander Louis C. Page and his back-seat radar in-
rcept officer (RIO), Lieutenant Commander John
. Smith, suddenly picked up four "bogies" 30 miles
head of their VF 21 F-4 Phantom and closing fast.
he pilot alerted his wingman, Lieutenant Jack E.
. Batson, and both aircraft readied their Sparrow
I air-to-air missiles. Within minutes, Page spotted
ur MiG-17 "Frescos" heading straight for the two
hantoms. As the highly maneuverable MiGs
anked, he squeezed off a missile. Hearing the Spar-
ow roar under him, Page pushed his F-4 up into the
ouds.

Almost simultaneously, Batson and his RIO,
ieutenant Commander Robert B. Doremus, fired
f another Sparrow and followed the flight leader
loft. Both missiles struck home; two MiG-17s ex-
loded in flame and smoke and spiralled to earth.
he remaining pair quickly turned tail and headed
or the safety of the Hanoi air space, offlimits to any
merican pursuers. When the two Phantom air
ews returned to *Midway*, they were surprised to
nd Secretary of the Navy Paul H. Nitze among the
eception committee. Nitze proudly announced the
rst American aerial victory of the Vietnam War
o the ship's company.

Three days later Navy pilots used skill, tactical
ngenuity, and just plain guts to score one of the
ost unusual MiG kills. Four prop-driven A-1H
kyraiders of VA 125 were flying to the site where
wo aviators went down when they received an
rgent radio call from destroyer *Strauss*. Her radar
ad picked up two hostile contacts closing fast on
he Skyraider flight. Soon, two MiG-17s circled in
ont of the Spads and then headed straight at them.
he enemy fired off air-to-air missiles as they
pproached.

Displaying great courage and coolness under fire,
ight leader Lieutenant Commander Edwin A.
reathouse kept his unit on course until the last mo-
ent and then led them on a sharp dive into a deep
alley. The hostile missiles missed their marks.
hen, to keep the enemy from attacking from below
r behind, Greathouse ordered the formation to level
ff at 500 feet and split in half. Each pair of Spads
ept turning in tight circles so that the MiGs could
ot move in on any one plane's vulnerable tail, or
six o'clock." Unable to break into the defensive

**Secretary of
the Navy Paul
H. Nitze
—When the
two victorious
Phantom crews
returned to
Midway he
happened to be
on board as
part of a tour
of inspection.
He announced
the news of the
MiG kills to the
carrier crew
over the public
address
system.**

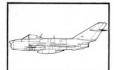

MiG-17 —The first enemy aircraft to be shot down by American aircraft. Although the "Fresco" (its NATO name) was based on a 1950 design it was lighter and more maneuverable though slower, than most comparable US aircraft it encountered in combat.

rings, the MiGs ripped off several more missiles from above, but they hissed harmlessly past the Skyraiders.

Then, the Americans turned the tables. Greathouse and his wingman worked one of the enemy jets into the cannon sights of the other pair of Spads, piloted by Lieutenant Clint Johnson and Lieutenant (j.g.) Charlie Hartmann. The fire from these planes mortally wounded the MiG, which hit the ground and exploded in flame. This was one of only two instances during the war when Navy prop-driven aircraft downed a jet.

The enemy soon got his licks in. What most military commanders had predicted finally happened on July 24. A surface-to-air missile site northwest of Hanoi, excluded from attack by Washington, fired a barrage of Soviet-made SA-2 Guideline missiles at a flight of Air Force F-105s. Suddenly, up through a "pea-soup" cloud cover came the 2½-ton "flying telephone poles," right at the formation. These weapons carried their 349 pounds of explosives as high as 60,000 feet in the air. Before the pilots could react, one missile disabled a fighter. The Air Force aviator ejected just in time to see his Thunderchief evaporate in a ball of fire. Although his life was spared, the pilot spent the next several years in North Vietnamese POW camps.

On August 11-12, the Navy suffered its first loss to the lethal SA-2. A pair of VA 23 Skyhawks on Midway were searching for trucks along a stretch of road 60 miles south of Hanoi. Lieutenant Commander Francis D. Roberge and Lieutenant (j.g.) Donald H. Brown, Jr., noticed two moving lights in the clouds about 15 miles from their position. Their mild curiosity soon turned to stark terror as the lighted objects followed the Skyhawks and then closed in on them. The pilots added speed and made evasive dives; they were not fast enough. Brown's plane lit up the dark night as it exploded. Roberge's aircraft also was hit but he coaxed the battered and burned attack bomber back to the carrier.

The fleet immediately took action to counter this convincingly demonstrated threat. On the 12th, Admiral Sharp, CINCPAC, ordered the establishment of Operation Iron Hand to concentrate forces against North Vietnam's SAM defenses. Carrier aircraft scoured the countryside in search of SA-2 batteries.

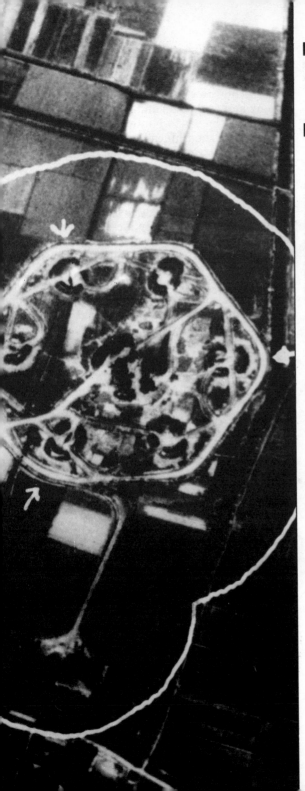

Rolling Thunder

An aerial reconnaissance photograph reveals a North Vietnamese SAM (surface-to-air) missile site near the port of Haiphong. The arrows indicate launch pads with SAMs in position. Each of these 35-foot two-stage supersonic rockets carried a 349-pound high-explosive warhead and was effective at homing in on aircraft flying at altitudes of between 3,000 and 60,000 feet.

Bombing on the railroad —these North Vietnamese railroad cars were blasted by two A-4 Skyhawks from *Oriskany*. The cars were spotted on a siding about 40 miles south of the Thanh Hoa bridge. The Skyhawks demolished five cars with 500-pound bombs just before this picture was taken. Later other aircraft returned to the siding and destroyed 20 of the other 25 railroad cars.

Once they spotted a site, carrier air units passed th information up the chain of command to Washingt and requested permission to strike it. Often as no by the time the okay reached Task Force 77, th enemy had packed up and moved the highly mobi SA-2s. Further, before late November 1965, SAN located near the Chinese border or in the Hanoi ar Haiphong restricted zones were invulnerable to a tack. In one instance, a carrier pilot discovered train near Hanoi transporting over 200 missile Commander Task Force 77, Rear Admiral Edwa C. Outlaw, immediately asked for authority destroy this unbelievably lucrative target. He w turned down. Soon, many of these same SA-2s joine the procession of "flying telephone poles" streakin skyward.

On August 12 and 13, 124 carrier aircraft, in larg formations, combed North Vietnam for these dea ly weapons. By sunset on August 13, "Black Fr day," none was discovered. To make matters wors antiaircraft guns had shot down five aircraft an damaged another seven.

The naval command decided to create special SA hunter-killer teams of two to five aircraft ready pounce on missile sites. After weeks of frustratin and fruitless searching, on October 17, a Navy tea found their elusive prey. An A-6 Intruder and fou A-4E Skyhawks from *Independence*'s Carrier A Wing 7 devastated a SAM battery at Kep, northeas of Hanoi. The attackers, dropping napalm bomb set one missile, three radar vans, and ten vehicle on fire. Another burning and disabled SA-2 slithere across the ground through the site adding to th destruction.

This "cat and mouse" game continued as th number of SAM sites increased, totalling 60 by th end of 1965. The Navy countered with new tactic Carrier aircraft increasingly attacked from a lo altitude, where the SAMs were least effective, an pilots learned to evade a missile by making shar high-speed maneuvers and diving for the deck to co fuse the SA-2's internal guidance system.

The Navy also called on the marvels of America science. In Project Shoehorn, sophisticated electron detection and warning devices, "black boxes," wer attached to naval fighter and attack aircraft. Th electronic countermeasures (ECM) equipmen monitored the radar frequencies of the enemy weapons. When it locked on to a SAM, the ECM gear gave off a loud, gong-like sound, warning the pilot of the fast-approaching missile. Few forgot that clarion call of danger.

Further, the Navy gave top priority to supplying Task Force 77 with stocks of the newly developed Shrike air-to-surface missile which homed in on the radar signal put out by a SAM site, following the beam right to its source.

Those and other measures limited the loss of Navy and Air Force aircraft. The communists launched over 184 SA-2s against American air units in 1965, but only 11 planes fell victim.

But the missile threat forced attack, flak suppression, and post-strike reconnaissance aircraft to approach targets from low altitudes, where the deadly antiaircraft defenses waited. The enemy's initial complement of antiaircraft artillery consisted of 1,500 37-millimeter and 57-millimeter antiaircraft guns, which were aimed by sight and only able to hit targets below 18,000 feet. But by the end of 1965, they boasted 5,000 weapons, including radar-guided 85-millimeter and 100-millimeter guns supplied by China and the Soviet Union. These latter weapons could bring down a plane from 45,000 feet. In addition, thousands of automatic weapons and even single-shot rifles carried by peasants in their rice fields were leveled at American aircraft.

As a result of this ominous buildup US losses began to mount. By August 1965, Seventh Fleet losses were averaging eight aircraft each month. By the end of the year 85 planes had gone down.

Task Force 77 also beefed up its power. In November *Kitty Hawk* came on line at Yankee Station carrying another squadron of versatile A-6 Intruders, flown by the "Black Falcons" of VA 85. In addition, the carrier deployed with a detachment of the new, technologically advanced E-2A Hawkeyes. These odd-looking turboprop planes, with a revolving radar dome mounted on top of the fuselage, were admirably equipped to guide naval strike forces to targets, warn of approaching MiGs, and relay messages. The Hawkeyes were the electronic eyes and ears of the carrier squadrons hitting North Vietnam.

On December 2, the nuclear navy joined the fight when *Enterprise* took her station off Vietnam. The

Survival gear —an oxygen mask, pistol, and flashlight were standard issue for pilots. The bulky survival vest had pockets for a compass, flares, first-aid kit, two survival radios and 15-inch knife. In an inside pocket a waterproof pouch contained plasticized survival maps and a "pointee-talkee" book with phrases in several languagues.

74,700-ton supercarrier operated more than 90 aircraft grouped into two F-4B Phantom and four A-4C Skyhawk squadrons, one KA-3B aerial tanker squadron, and detachments of RA-3B and RA-5C photo recce aircraft, E-1B and EA-3B electronic mission aircraft, and UH-2 helicopters. The "Big E" also carried a new system, the Integrated Operational Intelligence Center, which developed, interpreted, and distributed to the fleet the photographs and electronic intelligence collected by the RA-5C Vigilante.

With these powerful and technologically advanced ships, aircraft, and weapon systems available, Task Force 77 was ready to put them to work against the

Rolling Thunder

FLYING PANCAKE: With landing hook extended an E-2 Hawkeye early warning aircraft approaches *Kitty Hawk*. The twin-engined prop-jet with its 24-foot diameter long-range radar dome was used as an airborne control platform for both offense and defense. Once airborne, with its dome rotating at six rpm, the Hawkeye kept radar watch for MiG attackers, instantaneously assessing the enemy planes altitude, course, range and speed. The Hawkeye could also direct air strikes, guiding bombers to targets whose coordinates were known.

enemy. The opportunity came in December when President Johnson authorized the first strikes against industrial targets in the formerly sacrosanct Hanoi-Haiphong region. Chief among them was the Uong Bi thermal power plant, 15 miles northeast of Haiphong, which supplied 25 percent of North Vietnam's electrical power. On the 22nd, Task Force 77 launched a 110-plane Alpha strike against the plant with squadrons from *Enterprise*, *Ticonderoga*, and *Kitty Hawk*. In three waves, 30 minutes apart, the carrier air wings converged on the target. *Enterprise*'s Carrier Air Wing 9 attacked from the north while the *Kitty Hawk* and *Ticonderoga* squadrons moved in from the south. The "Big E" Skyhawks streaked in around 1500. North Vietnamese AAA threw up a wall of fire. Two A-4s in the first wave, hit at 3,000 feet, went down. Both pilots were lost. But the strike force overwhelmed the defenses.

The mass attack wreaked havoc on the power plant; the boiler house, generator hall, fuel storage complex, coal treatment facility, and 13 buildings were smashed or heavily damaged. Flames engulfed the site, oily black smoke rising hundreds of feet in the air.

Haiphong's electrical power was reduced by one-third and Hanoi's by one-fourth. The naval aviators showed how carrier forces could limit the enemy's warmaking ability.

This was the last Rolling Thunder mission of 1965, a year in which carrier forces flew 13,000 sorties over North Vietnam, dropped 64,000 bombs, and

PHOTO EVALUATION: An *Enterprise* photo intelligence interpreter scans film of enemy installations located along a river in Southeast Asia. Only hours before, one of the nuclear-powered carrier's RA-5C Vigilante aerial reconnaissance aircraft had returned the vital intelligence to the ship. As soon as the film was evaluated, the information was passed to *Enterprise* air wing's attack squadrons.

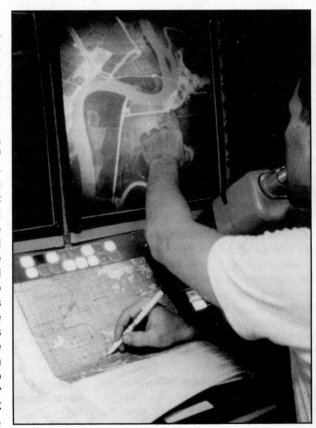

fired 128,500 rockets in the interdiction campaign.

On December 24, President Johnson ordered a temporary bombing halt for the Christmas holiday. He then extended the cease-fire and initiated a highly publicized peace offensive.

The communists rejected his overtures. The year-long bombing offensive did not bring the North Vietnamese to the negotiating table. Quite the contrary. The North Vietnamese used the 37-day bombing pause to rush supplies and reinforcements through southern North Vietnam and into the Ho Chi Minh Trail pipeline. An army of work parties repaired or rebuilt bridges, rail lines, and roads, and dispersed supplies into caves and underground storage sites. Worse yet, anticipating a resumption of Rolling Thunder, the North Vietnamese improved already strong air defenses. Another 18 early warning and fire control radar stations, over 400 antiaircraft positions, and 29 SAM sites sprang up over the North Vietnamese countryside. Key targets bristled with weapons.

When the president ordered continuation of the campaign against North Vietnam's lines of communication on January 31, the enemy was waiting. Attacks by *Kitty Hawk* and *Ranger* air units on bridges, rail lines, barracks, and fuel barges resulted in the loss of two Skyhawks and one Phantom. During the next three months, 42 naval aircraft went down over the North. April was especially bad, with 21 planes and 15 naval aviators lost.

Compounding Task Force 77's woes, the weather, always a hindrance to air operations in Southeast Asia, was particularly nasty during the first four months of 1966. The northeast, or winter, monsoon swept into the area with huge billowy clouds, often as low as 1,500 feet, rain squalls, and fog. Carrier units used short breaks in the weather to zoom in on targets approved in advance by Washington. Of course, the enemy concentrated his mobile defenses around these temporarily vulnerable sites. In general, these hit-and-miss operations were even less effective than the 1965 actions in reducing the flow of supplies south. By skillfully dispersing and camouflaging supply trucks and running them at night and in foul weather, the enemy was able to resupply forces in South Vietnam. Adding to the carriers' frustration over tight operational

Below decks —An approach controller monitoring the radar screen for incoming aircraft in the Approaches Center on board *Bon Homme Richard*. The positions of approaching aircraft were constantly updated and reported to the carrier's air officer, who was responsible for the launch and recovery of all planes.

restrictions, lousy flying weather, and deadly enemy defenses was the shortage of aerial ordnance and pilots. Early in the year, some "iron bombs" arrived at Yankee Station without essential components, such as fuses and tail assemblies. This forced carrier units to use other bombs that were too small, for example, to drop a bridge span into the river. This situation was short-lived as distribution of stocks from the United States, increased bomb production, and more efficient supply procedures pumped all types of needed ordnance into the fleet.

Concern over a shortage of aviators was prompted by the recognition that many pilots flew 16 to 22

THE WHALE:
An A-3B Skywarrior, the Navy's first all-jet attack plane, lifts off from the angled deck of a carrier to join an air strike over North Vietnam. During the early part of Rolling Thunder the Skywarrior, known as the "whale," was deployed as a pathfinder for other aircraft. When it was superseded by more advanced aircraft, the Navy version of this three-place light bomber was converted into an aerial tanker fitted with hoses, pumps and probes for in-flight refuelling and redesignated as the KA-3B.

missions each month, and some even 28. Morale dropped as men feared their "number" soon would be up. To ease this situation, the Navy shifted more aviators from stateside duty, increased the number of men accepted for pilot training, and limited tour lengths at Yankee Station. No man was required to serve more than two complete deployments in a 14-month period. Despite these measures to improve combat performance, the overall Rolling Thunder campaign was gradually losing steam by the spring of 1966. The year-long bombing program needed basic changes to cripple the enemy warmaking ability.

War in the Air

Crusaders v MiGs

N April 1966, the Seventh Fleet added greater punch to the air campaign. Task Force 77 was moved closer to North Vietnam as Yankee Station was shifted to 125 miles east of Dong Hoi at 17°30' north latitude and 108°30' east longitude.

The Navy and the Air Force also improved air operations by permanently dividing responsibility for the route packages. The Navy concentrated against the primarily coastal Route Packages 2, 3, 4, and 6B while the Air Force flew missions in 5 and 6A, the closest areas to its bases in Thailand. The MACV commander took charge of Route Package 1, just north of his I Corps battlefield in South Vietnam. This adjustment let naval aviators get intimately familiar with enemy targets, SAM sites, AAA "flak traps," and the geography of the coastal regions.

Almost immediately, losses fell. Nine carrier planes were shot down in May and another nine in June. While Task Force 77 lost 11 pilots, the SAR forces rescued the other seven.

Recovery of these men was aided by the establishment of North and South SAR stations between Yankee Station and the likely air avenues to and from the North Vietnamese coast. At each location, two destroyers monitored the radio frequencies of the naval air units over Southeast Asia and prepared to launch helicopters to rescue downed fliers.

At each station, one UH-2 Seasprite helicopter stayed on alert to pick up aviators who bailed out over land. Because of the lethal environment ashore, especially in North Vietnam, these aircraft were equipped with armor, self-sealing fuel tanks, and machine guns. Four larger SH-3A Sea Kings that

PUNCHING OUT:
Lt. Jack A.
Terhune
ejected when
his F-8E
Crusader's
engine flamed
out 20 miles
short of *Coral
Sea*. He is
directly above
the plane
seconds after
punching out.
His canopy has
flown
backwards over
his wingman.
Next Terhune's
drogue chute
deployed
(inset) and he
momentarily
floated over his
wingman, who
maintained
position to
direct search-
and rescue
teams.
Seconds later
the main chute
opened and
Terhune landed
in the water,
where he was
picked up
uninjured by
helicopter 80
seconds later.

flew from one of the carriers at Yankee Station were
similarly outfitted. The flattops also maintained
three unarmed and unarmored Seasprites for rescue
at sea. Air Force HU-16 amphibian aircraft and
HH-3E helicopters, the "Jolly Green Giants,"
operated in the Gulf of Tonkin as well. They saved
many Navy pilots.

The Navy's search and rescue forces were controlled by the SAR coordinator at the North SAR
Station. He guided the on-scene commander, who or

ited over the gulf with four Skyraider or Skyhawk
flak suppression aircraft. When a downed pilot or
his comrades still in the air called for help, the attack aircraft and the pickup helicopters dashed to
the crash or splash site. It usually took 20 to 30
minutes to snatch a flier from the sea after his plane
went in. A rescue took longer on land, if it could be
done at all.

The fleet would be in great need of the SAR force
as combat activity picked up. On April 13,

Ticonderoga air units got the mission to hit th[e] Haiphong Bridge, which carried the major highwa[y] from China into North Vietnam. The carrie[r] steamed as close as practical. Then, VA 144's CO[,] Commander David B. Miller, led his 11 A-4s an[d] four F-8 fighters of VF 53 toward the target fro[m] the north, where a ridge shielded the defenses unti[l] the last moment. Screaming over the ridge line, th[e] flight met two surface-to-air missiles head on. Th[e] jets dodged and weaved until they evaded the SA-[2] missiles. Resuming the attack run, the *"Tico"* unit[s] next faced intense flak. The enemy fire put a hol[e] in Miller's plane and damaged the Crusader of Com[-] mander Robair F. Mohrhardt, the VF 53 skipper[.] But the Americans pressed on. The Skyhawk[s] dropped their "eggs" right on target, splashing fiv[e] of the bridge's 21 spans.

Commander Mohrhardt, one of the pilots who fle[w] to the aid of destroyer *Maddox* on that fateful after[-] noon of August 2, 1964, nursed his burning Crusade[r] out to the gulf. There, he bailed out and was safel[y] scooped out of the water by the SAR force.

Then on the night of April 18-19 carrier unit[s] caught the enemy napping. The North Vietnames[e] had repaired and restored to operation the Uong B[i] thermal power plant northeast of Haiphong tha[t] Task Force 77 devastated at the end of 1965. It wa[s] due for a restrike.

Around midnight, Commander Ronald J. Hay[s]

nd his RIO, Lieutenant John T. Been, catapulted ff *Kitty Hawk* into the inky night sky. Right behind im came Lieutenant Eric M. Roemish and his back-seater". Hays, the CO of VA 85, led the two ntruders low over the water to escape North Vietnamese radar detection. The pair crossed the enemy oastline and within minutes streaked in on the arget. Uong Bi's antiaircraft guns were silent. Coming in separately, each Intruder "pickled off" 13 ,000-pound bombs and quickly disappeared into the arkness.

The power plant lit up like a Fourth of July display s electrical cables sent showers of sparks flying and uel erupted in multiple explosions. Reconnaissance hotos revealed that every one of the 26 "iron ombs" hit within the power plant enclosure, even nocking down its 250-foot smokestack. Complete urprise, achieved by careful planning at the fleet evel and skillful execution by veteran aviators, nabled two aircraft to accomplish what it took the Vashington-directed 110-plane strike to do the revious year.

In addition to these strikes on fixed installations, arrier aircraft continued to scour the North Vietamese landscape for targets of opportunity along he rail lines, roads, and coastal and inland aterways.

On one such occasion, Lieutenant William R. Vesterman and his bombardier/navigator, Lieutenant (j.g.) Brian E. Westin, were strafing barges in canal near Vinh when their A-6A was hit. The ilot, badly injured, lapsed into a semiconscious tate. At first, Lieutenant Westin helped Westerman uide the aircraft out to sea with oral instructions. But when the pilot grew progressively weak from is wounds, Westin flew the aircraft from his right eat by reaching over the mid-cockpit console. He lso radioed a Mayday. Once they were over the vater, Westin insisted that his comrade eject first. oon after the pilot punched out, the brave bombarier followed suit.

Within minutes an SH-3A Sea King arrived and etrieved Westin. He then directed the aircraft to Vesterman, who was too badly injured to get into he rescue sling. Westin jumped into the water, ecured his fellow officer in the sling, and signalled he helicopter pilot to rush Westerman to the SAR

Search and rescue —A UH-2 Seasprite helicopter moves off to starboard from *Franklin D. Roosevelt*. These fast, long-range utility helicopters, along with the heavier SH-3A Sea Kings, formed the core of the fleet's search and rescue force.

destroyer's medical aid station. Westin voluntaril
remained in the shark-infested water for anothe
SAR aircraft to pick him up. He was awarded th
service's highest honor—the Navy Cross.

In May and June, *Hancock*, *Kitty Hawk*, an
Ranger air squadrons attacked transportation an
industrial targets around Vinh, Thanh Hoa, Qu
Vinh, and Nam Dinh. *Hancock* units struck it ric
when they discovered a 25-car ammunition trai
near Phu Can. The bombed rolling stock explode
like a string of firecrackers.

AFTER THE FIRE:
Damage control
teams on *USS
Oriskany* put
out a blaze
started when a
magnesium
flare
accidentally
ignited in a
storage locker,
setting off
another 700
flares. Forty-
four men died,
including 25
aviators, as
flames and
smoke rapidly
swept below
decks.

June, however, was MiG month. American aircraft took part in 12 engagements with these Soviet-built interceptors. The North Vietnamese Air Force operated 70 aircraft, including the latest Soviet fighter, the MiG-21 "Fishbed". On the 12th, four MiG-17s jumped a flight of *Hancock* Crusaders flying combat patrol above an A-4 strike on enemy installations northwest of Haiphong. The jets slipped in under a 3,500-foot cloud ceiling and headed for the American aircraft. Commander Hal Marr, the CO of VF 211, and his F-8 pilots did not flinch.

Lt. (j.g.) Philip V. Vampatella —awarded the Navy Cross for destroying an enemy MiG even though his F-8E Crusader was flak-damaged and critically low on fuel.

Rather than breaking away and exposing their vulnerable six o'clock to the MiGs, the F-8 jocks flew straight into the North Vietnamese formation. The tactic worked. Outmaneuvering and outflying his opponent, Commander Marr fired off one Sidewinder. It missed. He quickly triggered of another that blew one MiG out of the sky. The surviving enemy pilots turned tail.

On June 21, VF 211 scored again. Marr's wingman, Lieutenant (j.g.) Philip V. Vampatella, a New Yorker from Long Island, was covering a downed flier along with other Crusader pilots. A they waited for the SAR helicopter, an antiaircraf burst rocked Vampatella's F-8E. The pilot didn' think the hit was serious but he was low on fuel, s he and his wingman headed for rendezvous with a aerial tanker.

Just then, one of the American pilots left behind broadcast a warning—"MiGs!" Vampatella and hi comrade came around and headed for the Crusade flight. By now he realized that his aircraft had been damaged by the flak. As he approached the battl between growing numbers of Crusaders and MiGs Vampatella saw one American jet go down i flames. Almost at the same time, another enem fighter closed on his tail. He dove straight for th deck at 600 knots. The damaged F-8 shuddered an bucked but came out of the dive when Vampatell pulled up just above the ground.

Looking around, the lieutenant saw that his pur suer had given up the chase and was heading home Although his fuel tank was now almost empty, Van patella did not thank his good fortune and make fo Hancock. He attacked. The pursued became the pur suer. The naval aviator crept up on the MiG's si o'clock and destroyed him with a Sidewinder. Ther the barely controllable and fuel-hungry Crusade limped out to a tanker and a further 60 miles to Han cock. Pilot and plane landed safely. For his dogge determination to stay in the fight, when other might have given up, Lieutenant (j.g.) Phil Van patella was awarded the Navy Cross.

By the spring, it was clear that despite the attack on bridges, railroads, and roads in southern Nort Vietnam, the enemy was still able to push supplie through to South Vietnam. This logistic effor however, was increasingly dependent on trucks an motorized boats and they needed fuel—lots of it. Reconnaissance discovered that 97 percent of North Vietnam's above-ground fuel supply was held in storage facilities at 13 locations. Destroy these stocks and the truck and boat fleet would slow to a crawl.

Admiral Sharp proposed this action early in 1966, but not until June did the Johnson administration quiet its fears that attacks on the petroleum, oil, and lubricants (POL) system would endanger civilians or bring on intervention by the communist powers.

Then, the Navy and the Air Force assigned air crews for these strikes—only the most experienced men. They were briefed and rebriefed to attack only in clear weather and to aim precisely at unmistakably military targets. North Vietnamese vessels in Haiphong harbor could not be attacked—even if they fired on the American planes first. Further, the strike planes could not bomb POL off-loading piers with tankers tied up to them.

Finally, on June 29, Task Force 77 and US Air Force units launched simultaneous attacks on POL facilities near Hanoi, Haiphong, and Do Son. While the US Seventh Air Force concentrated on the Hanoi site, *Ranger* and *Constellation* squadrons took on the other two.

Ranger's Carrier Air Wing 14 crossed the North Vietnamese coast with 28 attack, flak suppression,

UP IN SMOKE: Fuel storage tanks near Haiphong burn furiously after an attack in August 1966. In a three-month campaign, beginning on June 29, carrier aircraft destroyed most of North Vietnam's above-ground fuel storage facilities. The enemy resorted to storing fuel in underground tanks and 55-gallon drums dispersed throughout the countryside.

combat air patrol, Iron Hand, and photo recce aircraft. The A-4Cs of Commander Al "Shoes" Shaufelberger's VA 146 led the strike on North Vietnam's largest fuel facility at Haiphong. His "Blue Diamonds" delivered their general purpose bombs and rockets in neat rows on the fuel tanks which disintegrated in huge fireballs. Smoke from these infernos reached up into the sky and obscured the view of the following squadron, the "War Horses"

**CLEARED FOR
COMBAT:**
In the
deafening
noise of the
flight deck, a
flight director
clears a prop-
driven A-1
Skyraider for
takeoff while
an F-4
Phantom II
fighter lines up
to follow it
skywards. The
Skyraider was
the last aircraft
to fly from a
carrier that did
not require the
aid of a steam
catapult to
become
airborne.

of Commander Bob Holt's VA 55. These A-4Cs fur-
thered the immolation of the target. Meanwhile,
Commander Jim Brown's VF 142 Phantoms silenced
the heavy antiaircraft guns with bombs. An RA-5C
followed up and filmed the destruction of 95 percent
of the facility. The entire wing returned safely to
Ranger.

Meanwhile, *Constellation*'s Carrier Air Wing 15
struck the Do Son storage site, at the tip of a penin-

sula southeast of Haiphong. Here too, aircraft wreaked havoc, reducing the fuel tanks to cinders. No aircraft were lost.

Buoyed by the initial strikes, which knocked out over half of North Vietnam's storage capacity, Washington gave the green light for a full campaign against the fuel supply system. For the next two months, aircraft struck the ten remaining major storage facilities, restruck Hanoi and Haiphong, bombed fuel-carrying trains on the rail lines from China, and sought out smaller fuel dumps in the countryside.

On June 30 and July 1, *Hancock* and *Constellation* units smashed the POL tank farms at Bac Giang and Dong Nham, north of the Hanoi-Haiphong area. In succeeding weeks Task Force 77 squadrons kept the heat on Thanh Hoa, Vinh, and for the third time, Haiphong. They also attacked and sank half of the 600-ton barges used to transfer fuel from "neutral" tankers offshore to off-load facilities.

Steady hands —A member of *Bon Homme Richard*'s Explosive Ordnance Disposal team disarming a 250-pound bomb which broke loose from an A-4 Skyhawk as it launched for a combat mission over North Vietnam.

The North Vietnamese reacted furiously, concentrating air defenses around the remaining POL sites. When the American air units appeared over a likely target, as the enemy knew they would, they unleashed barrages of antiaircraft fire and volleys of SA-2 missiles. MiGs at still off-limits airfields nearby fought vigorously to defend the heartland. The United States lost more aircraft over the north in July than in any month since the start of Rolling Thunder 16 months before.

Even the North Vietnamese Navy, in hiding since the disastrous days of August 1964, put in an appearance. On the 1st of July three motor torpedo boats sortied against destroyers *Coontz* and *Rogers*, steaming at the North SAR Station. Before the PTs got to the ships, however, they were spotted by two *Constellation* F-4Bs, piloted by Lieutenant Commander Sven Nelson and Lieutenant Fred Miller. Almost at the same time, *Coontz* picked up the contacts on her radar. The call for air support went out.

Within 30 minutes, two Intruders, led by Lieutenant Commander Nels Gilette, arrived and zeroed in on the fast boats. Soon units from both "*Connie*" and *Hancock* joined the fray. They sank one boat. The other two launched torpedoes at a wishful thinking range, 12 miles from the destroyers, and hightailed it for home.

Their haste was in vain. The planes pursued them and then sent both of them to the bottom. The destroyers dashed to the scene and rescued 19 crewmen, the Navy's first North Vietnamese prisoners of war.

Despite the enemy's best efforts, by the end of August virtually all above-ground storage tanks and major pumping facilities lay blackened and in ruins. No Soviet tankers off-loaded at Haiphong in July. The following month communist ships delivered fuel only in fifty-five gallon drums. Other ships were diverted to China, where they offloaded bulk fuel for transshipment via railroad to North Vietnam. Further, a great number of fuel barges and railway tank cars lay twisted and scorched beside ripped up tracks.

Lt. (j.g.) William T. Patton —downed a MiG in his prop-driven Skyraider during a raid over Vietnam in October 1966.

In the final analysis, however, the POL campaign failed to deny the enemy the fuel he needed to keep moving supplies south. Since the beginning of Rolling Thunder, the North Vietnamese had been busy dispersing fuel throughout the country in small lots. Fifty-five gallon drums were placed along invulnerable village streets, in bunkered dumps, and in caves. The POL campaign caused short-term difficulties, but the communists soon adjusted and slogged on.

Already heavily committed to armed reconnaissance and strike operations in the north, Task Force 77's carrier forces needed reinforcement to carry out the POL campaign. In August, the carrier normally deployed off South Vietnam shifted to Yankee Station. After that, all carrier-based operations in Southeast Asia were launched from the Gulf of Tonkin. Then, three and sometimes four flattops steamed off North Vietnam.

To protect these vital ships and escorts from air attack and to control naval air operations in this hostile region, the Seventh Fleet set up a PIRAZ (Positive Identification Radar Advisory Zone) station southeast of Haiphong. From this spot, a cruiser equipped with the most advanced communications and radar kept track of all aircraft over North Vietnam and the northern half of the gulf. The ship's systems, which monitored hundreds of aircraft at once, enabled the on-scene commander to follow MiGs from takeoff to landing, vector US strike units and single aircraft to and from their targets, and

guide SAR and aerial refueling units to rendezvous
with American aircraft. The PIRAZ ship soon
became a vital link in Task Force 77's command and
control system.

Navigational accuracy was especially important
to the A-6 Intruders flying more and more night missions over the north. In one daring operation, on

War in the air

STINK BOMB: An A-1 Skyraider attack bomber is prepared for takeoff from the carrier *Midway* with a toilet bowl attached to one of its 15 bomb stations. Despite official denials, bomb shortages occurred and aircraft took off without full loads. One observer was reported to have seen an Air Force plane take off with a bomb on one wing and a concrete block as a counterbalance on the other. Later the bomb shortages were alleviated.

August 12, Lieutenant Commander Bernie Deibert and his B/N, Lieutenant Commander Dale Purdy, flying a lone A-6, caught the enemy napping. These naval officers of *Constellation*'s VA 65 streaked through some of the heaviest air defenses, dropped five 2,000-pound bombs precisely on the Hai Duong Bridge—knocking down the center span—and

Cmdr. Richard M. Bellinger —commander of Fighter Squadron 162 from *Oriskany* in jubilant mood in October 1966. He had just shot down a MiG-21, then the enemy's most advanced plane. Bellinger, who had been shot down in a Crusader by a MiG-17 three months earlier, destroyed the MiG-21 with two Sidewinder missiles from his F-8 Crusader.

headed out to sea before the communists sprang into action.

With most above-ground POL storage facilities destroyed by September, Rear Admiral David C. Richardson, Commander Task Force 77, concentrated his attacks against vulnerable segments of the transportation system. Naval units rained bombs on the rail yards at Ninh Binh, Thanh Hoa, and Phu Ly and destroyed bridges and tracks south of these rail centers. When supply trains backed up behind the destruction and the communists brought in trucks to unload them, aviators had a field day. Attack and fighter aircraft from *Constellation*, *Coral Sea*, *Oriskany*, and *Intrepid* strafed, rocketed, and bombed hundreds of immobilized locomotives, boxcars, tankers, and trucks during September and October.

While his comrades devastated the enemy below in October, Commander Richard Bellinger, CO of Fighter Squadron 162, cleared the sky of an especially menacing foe. On the 9th, Bellinger and three other F-8 pilots escorting attack aircraft from *Intrepid* were warned of approaching MiGs by a carrier alert plane.

Bellinger itched for a fight. The 42-year-old aviator piloted Army bombers in World War II and naval aircraft in Korea without chalking up an aerial victory. What's more, a MiG-17 shot down his Crusader in July.

The commander and his flight clawed their way up to 3,000 feet where they met the enemy. Bellinger zeroed in on one MiG which turned and tried to escape by rolling over and diving for the ground. The determined American followed. Closing on the desperately maneuvering MiG, Bellinger triggered off two heat-seeking Sidewinders. Within seconds the fighter exploded and scattered in fiery pieces over the landscape. Bellinger's victim was the first MiG-21, then the most advanced fighter in North Vietnam, shot down by the Navy.

While most carrier sailors never saw a MiG during the Vietnam War, they faced a more lethal enemy—fire. On the morning of October 26, this scourge struck *Oriskany* with a vengeance. When the day's scheduled strike mission was scrubbed because of poor flying weather, crewmen began returning bombs, rockets, gun ammunition, and other ordnance to the storage lockers below. A sailor handling magnesium flares accidentally ignited one of them. He threw it into the storage locker where it immediately set off between 600 and 700 other flares. Within seconds the fire touched off nearby stocks of ordnance.

Below deck spaces were soon filled with the screams and shouts of trapped and dying men. Many of the killed were pilots who only minutes before had been spared death or capture in North Vietnam when the attack was cancelled. A number of aviators, trapped in their staterooms, were asphyxiated.

Other sailors soon sprang into action. Damage control parties broke out fire hoses and began pumping tons of sea water into the blazing ship. Crewmen moved aircraft away from the fire and, at great risk of life, hauled over 300 bombs out of the inferno and threw them overboard. Their heroism prevented an even worse tragedy.

Still, when the crew of *Oriskany* finally beat back the flames and brought the situation under control, the loss was high. Forty-four men had died, including 25 aviators of Carrier Air Wing 16. The carrier air wing commander and two squadron executive officers were among the dead. Another 38 sailors were injured. Two helicopters, damaged beyond repair, were tossed over the side; four Skyhawks were heavily damaged. The wounded car-

INTELLIGENCE MACHINE:

A crewman in the modular combat information center (CIC) aboard *Oriskany* plots the position of an aircraft. The modular CIC was divided into glassed-off sections grouped around a central control area known as ''Display and Decision.'' Each module monitored one of the carrier's activities: air operations, air control, surface operations, electronic countermeasures, detection and tracking, carrier controlled approach, and weapons control.

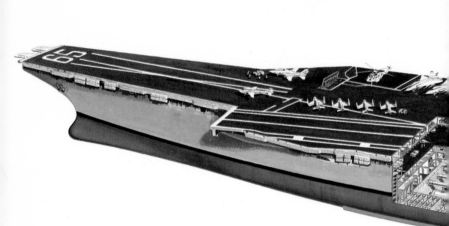

rier steamed to Subic and then San Francisco for major repairs and personnel replacements. She did not return to Yankee Station for eight months.

Even with temporary loss of *Oriskany*, the bombing campaign in North Vietnam continued. *Coral Sea*, *Oriskany*'s relief, *Enterprise*, *Kitty Hawk*, *Franklin D. Roosevelt*, and *Ticonderoga* spent the remainder of the year attacking key rail yards, depots, and defense facilities. On December 2, *Ticonderoga* and *Franklin D. Roosevelt* squadrons joined Air Force units in a 200-plane strike on the truck depot at Van Dien, just south of Hanoi. Evading 18 SAMs, the joint force devastated the site. A restrike 12 days later by these two carriers and *Kitty Hawk* completed the destruction of 75 percent of the repair, maintenance, and storage buildings.

As the northeast monsoon rolled over the Gulf of Tonkin, *Kitty Hawk*'s day-night, all-weather A-6 Intruders again came into their own. On the 11th and the 17th, using advanced navigation and aiming

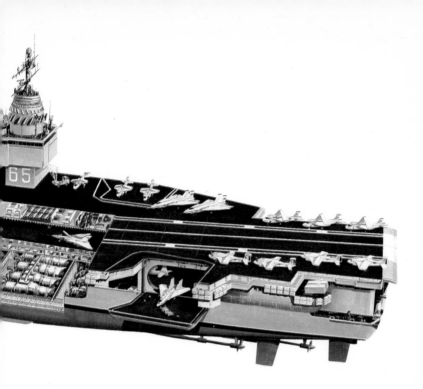

ns, they dropped heavy bomb loads on the SA-2 le assembly plant in Haiphong.

the time President Johnson ordered a 48-hour for the New Year holiday, the statistics for were in: Task Force 77 carried out 33,000 at-sorties against the North and more than 120 aft and 89 aviators had been lost in Southeast most over North Vietnam.

pite of the massive US interdiction campaign, ommunists showed no sign of giving up the gle. In fact, the enemy used the Christmas and Year's bombing halts to openly rush supplies einforcements through southern North Viet-

To some Navy reconnaissance pilots, the n's roads looked like the New Jersey Turnpike abor Day.

e these naval aviators, US leaders in the com-leater realized that after 22 months of opera-the American bombing campaign was not cut-off enemy supplies to the front.

**THE "BIG E":
With eight
water-cooled
reactors the
74,700-ton
Enterprise, the
first nuclear-
powered
aircraft carrier,
could, in
theory, cruise
for years
without
refuelling and
travel at better
than 30 knots.
It carried 5,000
men and ninety
aircraft.**

Shackles of War

Smart Bomb Raids on the North

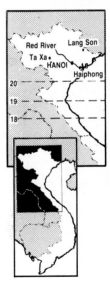

URING the early months of 1967, as the carriers
restled with the clouds and rain squalls of the
inter monsoon sweeping over the north, naval
aders pressed Washington to loosen the shackles
n combat operations. The no-nonsense commander
' US forces in the Pacific, Admiral Ulysses S.G.
harp, called for all-out attacks on the pillars of
orth Vietnam's warmaking structure: the key in-
ustries, electrical power generating plants,
etroleum storage sites, transportation support
cilities, military complexes, and air defense
stallations.

The Johnson administration authorized some
elaxation of bombing restrictions in 1967, but con-
nued to parcel out targets to the frustrated com-
at commanders: a power transformer station here,
cement plant or a few bridges there, one or two
mmunition dumps, a rail repair shop, or a truck
epot. Although the aerial attack units inched closer
nd closer to the centers of Hanoi and Haiphong,
neir efforts were piecemeal and diffused.

The carrier Navy, however, introduced new forces
nd weapons that promised to improve the effec-
veness of Rolling Thunder. Seventh Fleet
estroyers sortied against North Vietnamese coastal
raft and defense installations south of the 18th
arallel at the end of 1966. During the new year,
ne Navy permanently deployed a force of cruisers
nd destroyers off the communist mainland as far
orth as Thanh Hoa. These surface units, including
ne eight-inch-gun cruiser *Canberra*, roamed the
ast in packs of two to five ships in search of
'aterborne Logistics Craft (WBLC), known as
Wiblicks''. At other times, carrier-based A-1
kyraider and S-2 Tracker spotting planes assisted

93

in shelling coastal roads, rail lines, bridge ferry crossings. The gun ships kept up a dead test with coastal batteries, which hit 19 shi ing 1967 and 1968. However, not one of the in this operation, code-named Sea Dragon, was

The Seventh Fleet also began using air-dr mines to strengthen the anti-infiltration effor Navy kicked off a new phase on February 26, Commander A.H. Barie led six of his *Enterpri* tack Squadron 35 Intruders low over the sea ar the mouths of the Ca and Giang rivers. Once the A-6As "pickled off" their mines and retur the safety of the gulf.

The following month, *Kitty Hawk* aircraf another three minefields in the mouths of th Kien, and Cua Sot rivers. These Intruder proached their drop zones at night and in weather. Nonetheless, the A-6 pilots laid thei nance in the precise patterns required of mine After losing several vessels, the enemy swe

Shackles of War

FLYING GAS STATION:
A KA-3B Skywarrior aerial tanker refuels a trailing Skyhawk attack plane enroute to a target in North Vietnam. Mid-air refuelling increased the range and time on station of naval aircraft over Southeast Asia and enabled many fuel-starved planes to cover the last few miles home to their carriers.

me of the mines, but for a time the waterways ere closed to coastal traffic. In later months Task orce 77 aircraft dropped thousands more of these eapons along inland waterways and on the land pproaches to bridges and ferry crossings in the anhandle.

Another new weapon was the TV-guided Walleye lide bomb. Pilots selected the target, locked a TV e onto it, and released the 1,000-pound bomb. Even the aviator banked away to avoid flak or SAMs, e Walleye would unerringly seek out the target. Rear Admiral Thomas J. Walker, Commander arrier Division 3, chose Commander Homer Smith, O of *Bon Homme Richard*'s VA 212, to baptize the Valleye in combat. This veteran aviator flew his Valleye-armed A-4 Skyhawk, escorted by four Phanms, against the barracks at Sam Son on March 11. fter the approach, Smith released the glide bomb nd joined the other pilots observing its descent. The Valleye went right through the window of its target

Keeping track —a crewman in Primary Flight Control aboard the attack carrier *Bonne Homme Richard* records up-to-the-minute data on launches and recoveries. With the carriers frequently averaging more than 100 combat sorties a day—the record was 165 held by *Enterprise*— accurate and instant information on the whereabouts of planes was vital.

and exploded inside, demolishing the building. Th day and the next Commander Smith and his co rades from *"Bonnie Dick"* dropped more of the "smart bombs" on other barracks and on the P Dien Chau and Thanh Hoa bridges. They scor direct hits every time.

In fact, 65 of the 68 experimental Walley dropped by the carrier air wing during the shi seven- month deployment in the Western Pacific i pacted on target. The day of precision guided mu tions (PGM) had arrived.

Meanwhile, other squadrons carried out tra tional attacks on the targets released Washington, including the Thanh Hoa rail yard a the Hon Gay thermal power plant and boat rep facility. In addition, on five nights during Marc carrier air units for the first time struck the Th Nguyen industrial complex north of Hanoi.

President Johnson also authorized air attacks key electrical power generating facilities. On Ap 20 multicarrier Alpha strikes crippled Haiphong two thermal power plants, dousing the lights in th port and in nearby Hon Gay for several nights.

The following month Task Force 77 launched m jor bombing raids on the power plants at Bac Gia and Uong Bi and, for the first time, the capita 32,000-kilowatt generating plant in the middle downtown Hanoi.

For the sensitive Hanoi operation, Washingt wanted the Navy to use the now-proven Walle glide bomb. To ensure a precision attack on th target, in a heavily populated residential section, t Navy once again selected as strike leader the co Commander Homer Smith.

On the afternoon of May 19, Smith's A-4 and th of his wingman, Lieutenant Mike Cater, catapult from *"Bonnie Dick"*. A Walleye hung undernea each Skyhawk.

The pair was soon joined by six F-8E Crusade for flak suppression and fighter escort. As *Kit Hawk's* diversionary force struck the Van Di truck depot south of the capital, Smith's group rac at tree-top level across the countryside, dodging a tiaircraft fire and SA-2 missiles. Still unscathed, t commander and his wingman streaked over Hano rooftops, identified their target, released t 1,000-pound Walleyes, and turned for home.

The bombs found their mark. John Colvin, the resident British consul, observed that moments after the two Skyhawks broke off their run, smoke and flame rose from the site of the power station and the ceiling fan in his apartment stopped dead. Traveling to the generating facility, Colvin found the 100-foot-high main building holed by the blast of the explosives and its two smokestacks in piles of rubble. His admiration for the accuracy and destructiveness of the attack was equalled only by his respect for the resourcefulness of the North Vietnamese—electricity was restored to Hanoi the next day.

Along with the electrical power network, President Johnson approved attacks on a key component of North Vietnam's air defense system, the MiG bases. On April 24, over two years since the start of air combat operations over the North, *Kitty Hawk* squadrons carried out the first attacks on the enemy's "in-country sanctuaries".

Carrier squadrons also struck the airfield at Kep, 37 miles northeast of Hanoi. They pitted the main

SMART BOMB:
A Walleye glide bomb, one of the "smart" weapons introduced in the '60s, attached to an Intruder during tests prior to delivery to Vietnam. When dropped by a cool, experienced pilot, the precision-guided Walleye was deadly accurate against fixed targets.

Shackles of War

BASE ATTACK: A-4 Skyhawks from *Oriskany* conduct an air strike against the Kien An airfield and surrounding revetments five miles southwest of Haiphong. Beginning in April 1967, attacks like these against the enemy's air defense system represented a significant escalation in combat operations.

runway with craters, damaged several fighters o the ground, and shot down four MiG-17s that ros to the challenge. The Navy lost two Crusaders.

The enemy response was fierce. From late Apr to the end of May, its air force swarmed all over th Hanoi-Haiphong-Thanh Hoa "Iron Triangle" i search of American aircraft.

On May 1 a MiG-17 jumped Lieutenant Te Swartz of VA 76 over Kep airfield. The America

was busy rocketing parked aircraft with his
Skyhawk when the fighter came up on his six
o'clock. Swartz's wingman broadcast a warning. The
skilled Swartz immediately rolled his highly
maneuverable "Scooter" and soon found his sights
lined up on the tail of the overshooting MiG. React-
ing instinctively, Swartz fired off his Zuni rockets—
normally air-to-surface weapons—and destroyed the
aerial foe. The attack pilot's *Bon Homme Richard*

shipmates added to the tally on the day that Commander Homer Smith carried out his daring raid on the Hanoi power plant. Before that attack was over, Lieutenant Phil Wood of VF 24 shot down a MiG-17.

As Commander Smith and his wingman departed the target area and headed for the hills to the southwest, ten angry MiGs streaked after them. They intercepted the two A-4s and their four F-8 protectors southwest of Hanoi. In a scene reminiscent of the World War II Battle of Britain, the 16 jets dived, turned, and rolled in an aerial melee.

The Americans came out on top. In quick succession, the commanding officer of VF 211, Commander Paul Speer, and his wingman, Lieutenant (j.g.) Joe Shea, blasted MiG-17s out of the sky. Soon afterward VF 24's Lieutenant Bobby Lee flamed another one. Seeing that the American A-4s were out of reach and having already lost four aircraft, the North Vietnamese gave up the chase. Thus ended one of the Navy's largest air-to-air engagements of the war.

The communists, however, exacted a price for American successes. Antiaircraft weapons filled the air with deadly fire, rivalling that over Germany in World War II for intensity. In July the enemy also targeted a record 233 missiles against naval aircraft. Nineteen carrier planes fell victim to SA-2s and AAA fire that costly month.

In the face of this growing defensive strength, the Navy's SAR forces made heroic efforts. An SH-3A Sea King, crewed by Lieutenant Neil R. Sparks, Lieutenant (j.g.) Robin Springer, and Petty Officers Masengale and Ray, evaded enemy fire for over two hours before plucking Lieutenant Commander Demetrio A. Verich from an area south of Hanoi crawling with the enemy.

Unfortunately, rescue attempts in the heavily defended North Vietnamese heartland often failed, sometimes at great cost. Two days after Verich's pickup, an *Oriskany* A-4E crashed south of the capital. The first helicopter on the scene, an SH-3A off *Hornet*, was punctured by gunfire. One aviator was killed. A second "rescue bird," from guided missile destroyer *Worden*, had its wings clipped when ground fire damaged its main and tail rotors. The next helicopter dispatched, a Sea King, was shot down with the loss of all four crewmen. Completing the day's sad tally, the enemy knocked down an

Utility rocket —An aviation ordnanceman adjusts the fins of a five-inch Zuni rocket. Although designed as an air-to-surface weapon, a Zuni was used by Lt. Ted Swarz, flying a Skyhawk, to down a MiG-17. The Zuni is being adjusted in the *Midway*'s main dining room, which doubled as a bomb-assembly area before missions.

A-4E escorting the SAR force. The pilot punched out over the gulf. Destroyer *Richard B. Anderson*'s boat fetched him from the water. Thus, despite the extraordinary courage and determination of SAR personnel, they could not retrieve the unlucky *Oriskany* pilot. He was to die in captivity.

There was no letup in the duel with death in the skies over the North. On July 21, Crusaders from *Bon Homme Richard* tangled with eight MiG-17 "Frescos" near the petroleum storage facility at Ta Xa. In a short, sharp fight, Fighter Squadron 24's Commander Marion H. "Red" Isaacks and Lieutenant Commander Robert L. Kirkwood destroyed a MiG apiece with a Sidewinder missile and 20-millimeter cannon fire. Lieutenant Commander Ray Hubbard, Jr., of VF 211, flamed another with a Zuni air-to-surface rocket and gunfire.

Celebrations were short-lived, however, for on the 29th, Task Force 77 suffered its worst loss of the war. On that bloody day, *Forrestal* exploded in smoke and flame.

The supercarrier had just arrived at Yankee Station, following extensive overhaul and modernization work in the United States, to begin her first—and last—combat tour of the Vietnam War. Late in the morning the *Forrestal*'s Phantoms, Skyraiders, and Vigilantes prepared to take off for the second air strike of the day. Planes were fully armed and fueled.

At the worst possible time, a Zuni rocket carried by an F-4 was somehow triggered. The missile impacted squarely on the fuel tank of an A-4E parked forward of the Phantom. In an instant, the aft end of the flight deck erupted in explosions and fire fed by volatile jet fuel, bombs, and rockets. Sailors were knocked into the sea by the blast. In below-deck spaces, men were asphyxiated by the oxygen-consuming blaze.

Disregarding exploding ordnance and intense fire, crewmen rushed into the conflagration to detach bombs from aircraft and toss them overboard. Many bluejackets made repeated trips across the exposed deck. One man, seeing an "iron bomb" about to "cook off," grabbed a fire extinguisher and raced over to the site. Just as he got there, the bomb exploded in a thunderous blast, killing him and other men nearby.

On camera —*Bon Homme Richard* attack aircraft race down the Thai Binh river as their bombs blast targets in the My Xa area near Haiphong on July 19, 1967. The action was filmed by an unarmed reconnaissance plane which had the dangerous but routine responsibility of following attack units and bringing back photos for bomb damage assessment.

FIRE FIGHT:
As an SH-3A Sea King helicopter prepares to deliver fire-fighting equipment, crewmen work desperately to stop the spread of fire on the *Forrestal* on July 29, 1967. The fire began when an F-4 Phantom accidentally fired a Zuni rocket hitting armed and fueled aircraft on the flight line. The escort destroyer *Rupertus* (inset) was first on station to help fight the 12-hour fire that killed 134, injured 59 others, destroyed 21 aircraft and damaged 43 others.

The stricken carrier's escorts, destroyers *Ruper-is* and *George K. MacKenzie*, pulled alongside. heir fire hoses joined those of *Forrestal* in pouring 2a water on the aft section. The carrier's Task Force 7 sisters, *Oriskany*, *Bon Homme Richard*, and *In-epid*, assisted with fire-fighting equipment, casual-evacuation helicopters, and medical treatment. lospital ship *Repose* raced north from her station ff South Vietnam to take on the injured and the ead. A total of 134 officers and men were killed and nother 60 required hospitalization.

When the last fires were extinguished below, after

Damage assessment — A section of the flight deck of the *Forrestal* ripped apart by the fire and explosions of July 29, 1967. The damage, estimated then at $72 million, was so extensive that the ship was forced to return to the United States for extensive repairs and replacement of her destroyed and damaged aircraft.

12 hours of valiant effort, the burned and broken hulks of 62 destroyed and damaged aircraft littered the flight deck. Damage to the ship was extensive, ending the supercarrier's brief combat tour. She steamed for home.

Even without *Forrestal*, Task Force 77 continued the increasingly fierce aerial assault on North Vietnam. In late July and early August *Oriskany* pilots celebrated the previous year's successes against the North Vietnamese Navy by sinking or damaging three enemy PT boats tied up along the shore.

With flying weather perfect during most of August, *Constellation*, *Oriskany*, and *Intrepid* launched major strikes against targets close to the border with China, including the Lang Son railroad bridges, Na Phuoc railroad yard, and Van Hoa naval base. At Van Hoa, *Intrepid*'s Carrier Air Wing 10 carried out two Alpha strikes three hours apart.

While dodging 51 SAMs on the 21st, Carrier Air Wing 14 squadrons off *Constellation* cratered the runway at Kep airfield and destroyed one enemy plane on the ground. The attack on Kep and the Duc Noi rail yard cost "*Connie*" three VA 196 Intruder aircraft.

Also on the 21st, Seventh Fleet air units returned to the Hanoi thermal power plant. Since the May strike by Commander Homer Smith it had been repaired and ringed with antiaircraft and SAM sites. Undeterred, *Oriskany*'s VA 163 A-4Es guided their five Walleye glide bombs right into the generator hall and boiler house, demolishing the complex. Even though the air was filled with lead, the flight safely dodged and weaved through the fire and streaked out to sea. When the unit touched down on *Oriskany*, Commander James B. Busey found 12 bullet and shrapnel holes in his aircraft.

Busey was lucky. August had witnessed the loss of 16 aircraft and many crews. SA-2s knocked down six planes, a new monthly record. The North Vietnamese had sent 249 SAMs aloft, 80 on the 21st alone.

Still, the Americans pressed the attack and at the end of August, Task Force 77 began a campaign to cut Haiphong off from the interior. Fearing damage to foreign shipping in the port, through which passed 85 percent of North Vietnam's imported war materials, Washington would not allow the Navy to lockade or mine the narrow approaches to the city. As an alternative, the Johnson administration okayed strikes against bridges around Haiphong.

On August 30, 24 aircraft from *Oriskany* worked their way through 37-, 57-, and 85-millimeter AAA fire and a number of "flying telephone pole" missiles to hit the major Haiphong highway bridge south of the port. They dropped their "iron bombs" neatly on the structure. Three of the four spans collapsed into the water.

Within weeks, every one of the major bridges around Haiphong was down, but the seemingly untiring work parties soon repaired them. Traffic again began to move out of the port. Not to be outdone, Task Force 77 returned in October and demolished spans of these same four bridges.

Meanwhile, the Navy's air combat units sought out the dredges that kept the harbor and river approaches free of silt. Without their services, the Haiphong waterways became increasingly difficult for communist bloc ships to navigate. Lightering cargo in from offshore vessels was not an attractive alternative.

The effort to interdict the supply lines out of Haiphong took effect in September and October. Supplies, over 200,000 tons, piled up in storage lots all over the city. During one 2-day period, enemy antiaircraft fire slackened considerably and no SAMs were fired at American aircraft flying overhead. Apparently, stocks of high-priority munitions were running low.

The carriers turned the heat up even more. On October 12 Commander Elbert Lighter led an *Oriskany* Alpha strike right into central Haiphong against the shipyard. They dove on the riverside complex, sinking five barges and one motorized boat and destroying maintenance and repair shops. Right after that, *Intrepid* units wrecked ship and boat yards in the harbor area. Attack squadrons tore up marine railways, shipways, and other facilities supporting port operations.

As these multi-aircraft flights wreaked havoc around Haiphong, single A-6 Intruders concentrated on prime targets. On October 30, Lieutenant Commander Charles B. Hunter and his bombardier/navigator, Lieutenant Lyle F. Bull, carried out a daring attack on the Hanoi railroad ferry slip.

Weather assessment —An aerographer's mate plots a weather chart aboard *Hancock*. August 1967 was an exceptional month with perfect weather every day. Conditions off Yankee Station were worst in the monsoon season when the rain was constant.

HUNTER-KILLER:
A Vought A-7 Corsair II, first deployed to Vietnam on the *Ranger* in December 1967, prepares to take off from *Constellation*. The Corsair II could deliver 15,000 pounds of bombs on target regardless of weather, thanks to its then state-of-the-art continuous-solution navigation and weapons systems.

The Intruder crew, from *Constellation*'s VA 196, used electronic navigation systems to fly through the black night. Staying as low as possible to avoid SAMs, they maneuvered the plane over and around the jagged karst ridges commanding the approaches to the target. The plane was only 18 miles from the capital when Hunter's "black box" picked up signals from a missile radar site. They were detected!

The pilot immediately dove for the ground; Bull began programming his electronic bombing gear. Then another SA-2 site locked onto the Intruder. Again, Lieutenant Commander Hunter headed for

he treetops at more than 450 knots. Within seconds
hey saw it—the flame of an SA-2 missile's exhaust
it up the darkness as it streaked towards them. The
ilot rolled to port and the aircraft dropped to 2,000
eet, upside down. The maneuver worked; the SAM
xploded harmlessly 200 feet away.

Hunter righted the A-6 and pressed on. By now
ntiaircraft fire laced the sky, casting an unearthly
low on the land below. Both men spotted SAMs con-
erging: three to port and two more to starboard.
ided by the light of bursting AAA shells and
nemy searchlights, the pilot flew the jet just off the

Arming up —An ordnanceman trundles several 250-pound bombs across *Hancock*'s flight deck for loading on the carrier's attack aircraft. The bombs will not be fused until shortly before the mission starts.

ground for the last seven miles to the target. This risky but skillful move disoriented the missiles tracking systems and they exploded out of range although close enough to rock the A-6. The Intruder's bombing device released eighteen 500-pound bombs at the precise moment. At the same time, Hunter executed a hard G turn to starboard to evade the last of that night's 16 SA-2s fired at the aircraft. As they passed out of harm's way Lieutenant Commander Hunter and Lieutenant Bull watched their bombs obliterate the railroad ferry ship on the bank of the Red River.

On December 3, *Ranger* deployed to Yankee Station carrying aircraft that, like the remarkable A-6 were advanced, all-new-design jets. The Vought A-7A Corsair II, flown by VA 147, could deliver 15,000 pounds of bombs with state-of-the-art navigation and weapon systems.

As this newcomer was introduced, the veteran Skyraiders, Skyhawks, Intruders, Crusaders, and Phantoms of Task Force 77 continued to bear the operational burden over the North. Rotating in and out of the gulf during November and December, *Constellation*, *Coral Sea*, *Intrepid*, *Oriskany*, *Kitty Hawk*, and *Ranger* attacked the ship and boat yards storage and administrative buildings, and barge facilities near Hanoi and Haiphong. Simultaneously, units worked over the rolling stock, rail lines, and switching yards in the Iron Triangle between Hanoi Haiphong, and Thanh Hoa.

By the end of 1967, the bombing campaign had severely damaged the transportation system that supplied communist forces fighting in South Vietnam and Laos. That year, Task Force 77 air units knocked down 955 bridges, damaged 1,586 others, and devastated large segments of the rail and road network. In addition, the Seventh Fleet's air squadrons and shore bombardment ships destroyed more than 700 trucks, 400 pieces of rolling stock, and 3,200 coastal and river craft.

Further, cargo operations at Haiphong were hampered by the naval effort to isolate the strategic port. Heavy enemy losses of harbor lighters and trucks considerably increased the time it took to unload ships and to move their munitions out of the area.

To sustain the aerial campaign, the carrier's brave

viators wiped out almost 200 antiaircraft batteries, 0 SAM sites, and 46 MiGs in the air and on the round.

The cost to the Navy was high. In 1967, 133 aircraft were shot down and two-thirds of their crews ere killed or captured.

What was worse the North Vietnamese surmounted all the obstacles thrown up by the bombing campaign. Thousands and thousands of men, omen, and even children labored nightly repairing bridges, roads, and rail lines; transporting munitions by sampan, barge, and bicycle; and constructing bypasses through the cratered and scorched andscape of southern North Vietnam. At the end f 1967 adequate supplies of arms, ammunition, and ther war material were reaching the enemy's jung-ed redoubts in South Vietnam.

The communist logistic picture brightened even more during the 24-hour Christmas and 36-hour New Year's bombing halts ordered by President ohnson in late 1967. While American leaders aited in vain for the communists to respond to this nilateral restraint, Hanoi openly rushed troop reinforcements and munitions south. Thousands of supply trucks, often bumper to bumper, sped toward the ntrances to the Ho Chi Minh Trail as American econnaissance pilots disgustedly witnessed the round-the-clock surge.

The reason for this buildup was soon apparent. On anuary 31, Viet Cong units emerged from their ungle and urban hideouts to launch a nationwide ssault against South Vietnam's cities.

The carriers at Yankee Station shifted the emphasis of attack to South Vietnam and, to a lesser xtent, to Laos, during the first three months of 968. Nonetheless, Task Force 77 continued to aunch Alpha strikes and single-plane operations gainst the North whenever the weather ooperated—as it often did not. During January and 'ebruary, visual bombing was possible on only 3 per-ent of the days. The weather was little better in March.

Navy flyers used innovative tactics to get at the nemy whenever the northeast monsoon abated. On wo separate occasions during the first week of anuary, carrier pilots used Sidewinder air-to-air nissiles against trains. On the 2nd, Commander

Bridge tally—By the end of 1967, carrier units had destroyed or damaged in excess of 2,500 bridges in an attempt to disrupt the North Vietnamese warmaking effort. Here the western span of the Loc Dinh Highway Bridge has been destroyed by aircraft from *Constellation*. The four-span two-lane bridge was ten miles from China and 83 miles northeast of Hanoi.

Shackles of War

EMERGENCY LANDING: Navy pilot Lt. (j.g.) Denny Earl, both legs shattered by antiaircraft fire, successfully manages to land his damaged A-4 Skyhawk on the deck of the carrier *Oriskany* thanks to the nylon emergency barrier. It served as a fail-safe and assured the pilot that he would not have to make more than one landing attempt if his plane missed the arresting wire.

Charles A.L. Swanson of *Oriskany*'s Fighter Squadron 162 knocked out the locomotive of a 45-car train with a heat-seeking Sidewinder. Other air units then obliterated the stationary train. Several days later, his squadron mate, Lieutenant Commander John S. Hellman, repeated this feat.

At the end of January, Task Force 77 aircraft again struck a much-attacked but little-damaged target—the Ham Rong or Dragon's Jaw highway

and railway bridge at Thanh Hoa. Since the first attack on the truss bridge in 1965, Navy, Air Force, and Marine air units had flown more than 700 sorties against it, dropping more than 12,000 tons of bombs and rockets. Still it stood, almost impervious to damage. And the forest of enemy antiaircraft guns, automatic weapons, and SAMs guarding the Ham Rong Bridge shot down eight American planes.

When *Coral Sea*'s Carrier Air Wing 15 struck once

Lt. Cmdr. Michael J. Estocin — awarded a posthumous Medal of Honor for his gallantry while serving with Attack Squadron 192 over North Vietnam on April 20 and 26, 1967.

more on the 28th of January, the result was the same. VA 153 and VA 155 aircraft dropped 2,000-pound bombs precisely on target—leaving the bridge holed and damaged, but standing. In little over a week, logistic traffic again passed over the repaired structure.

The three-year-long effort to destroy the Thanh Hoa bridge symbolized Rolling Thunder. Despite the courage and skill of US aviators, the most advanced weapons that American science and industry could develop, and innovative tactics, the enemy's lines of communication to the South were not cut.

However, his industrial and transportation infrastructure took a terrible beating and reinforcements and supplies were often delayed. But enough support got through to sustain combat forces and even to launch major offensives. Further, this aerial campaign cost the United States dearly.

The Navy suffered the loss of 283 aviators killed, captured, or missing, the destruction of more than 300 aircraft, damage to 1,000 others, and expenditure of tons of costly ordnance.

Recognizing the failure of his strategy in Southeast Asia and the diminishing return from bombing, President Johnson halted attacks against targets in North Vietnam above the 20th parallel on March 31 and announced his decision not to seek reelection in November.

Between April 1 and November 1, 1968, Task Force 77 continued to attack supply lines between the 18th and 19th parallels. The objective now was purely military: to interdict North Vietnamese lines of communication in the narrow panhandle with a massive concentration of firepower.

Cruisers and destroyers of the Sea Dragon force shelled targets along the coast, sinking enemy Wiblicks foolish enough to traverse these dangerous waters. Carrier aircraft mined and bombed ferry crossings, rail and road bridges, truck parks, supply and fuel dumps, and inland waterways. In unceasing day and night attacks, the fleet reduced logistic traffic flow to a trickle. This seven-month interdiction effort ended the Rolling Thunder campaign.

On November 1, an unearthly quiet settled on the North Vietnamese countryside as the American air forces shifted their deadly attention to Laos and South Vietnam.

Shackles of War

CENTER OF OPERATIONS:

In the center of a cold windy deck, a catapult officer coordinates the launching of aircraft from *Bonne Homme Richard*. A nearby console monitored pressure levels from the eight boilers that provided steam for the four catapults. Attempting to launch a plane with insufficient pressure was known as a "cold shot" and could be fatal if the plane failed to gain enough speed, and, instead of taking off, dribbled into the sea.

Stopping the Flow

CHAPTER

5

Attacks on Laos and South Vietnam

THE Navy's air war against North Vietnam made the big headlines during the Southeast Asian Conflict, but almost as important to the allied effort were its actions in South Vietnam and Laos, where carrier units directly assisted infantrymen on the ground.

Carrier squadrons also continued the campaign to interdict enemy reinforcements and supplies by visiting fire and fury on base camps and storage sites in the interior of South Vietnam and on the Ho Chi Minh Trail. Largely unsung, the naval aviators who fought in South Vietnam and Laos did so with great skill and determination to help their American and Asian comrades locked in combat with Viet Cong, Pathet Lao, and North Vietnamese forces.

This desire was evident in March 1965 when the Navy responded to the request of General Westmoreland, the MACV commander, for carrier air support against the in-country foe. Following a meeting on board flagship *Ranger* between the general and Rear Admiral Henry L. Miller, Commander Task Force 77, Washington leaders gave the go-ahead to strike operations in the Republic of Vietnam.

The carriers joined the fight in South Vietnam on April 15 when *Midway*, *Coral Sea*, and *Yorktown* steamed to a point off the coast, turned into the wind, and catapulted aircraft. The Navy and US and South Vietnamese air forces levelled a Viet Cong base camp and logistic complex in War Zone C northwest of Saigon.

As in the opening months of the Korean War, the Navy's movable airfields filled the bill for air support in the initial phase of the Vietnam conflict. While the Pacific Command constructed airfields in

115

South Vietnam and Thailand for shore-based Air Force and Marine units, the Seventh Fleet rotated carriers to an operational staging area offshore. This position, named Dixie Station to differentiate it from the northern site, was located southeast of Cam Ranh Bay at 11° north latitude, 110° east longitude.

Usually, when an aircraft carrier deployed to the Western Pacific it operated first at Dixie Station to break in green aviators and commanders. The enemy's antiaircraft weapons in South Vietnam were not as numerous or effective as those found in the Red River Delta or panhandle regions of North Vietnam. Still, the enemy shot down 14 fighter, attack, and reconnaissance planes over the South during the 16 months Dixie Station existed.

Rear Adm. Henry L. Miller —commanded the Seventh Fleet's powerful Task Force 77 during the momentous air operations against North Vietnam in the early months of 1965.

The enemy suffered much greater losses in men and material. Flying one-third of all sorties in the South, the naval air units at Dixie Station levelled hundreds of Viet Cong ammo dumps, bunkers, and jungle storage huts and shot up numerous sampans carrying troops and munitions. Carrier squadrons often broke up ambushes, beat off ground attacks, and chased Viet Cong forces back into their jungle hideouts.

This support helped South Vietnamese and American ground units prevent the complete loss of the US Army Special Forces camp at Dong Xoai, northeast of Saigon in War Zone D. Close to midnight on June 9, 1965, two Viet Cong regiments opened a 200-round mortar barrage and stormed through the outer perimeter wire. Through the long night, Army Green Berets, South Vietnamese irregulars, and nine men of the Naval Mobile Construction Battalion Team 1104, better-known as SEABEES, engaged the enemy guerrillas at close quarters.

At dawn, the battle still raged. One SEABEE, Construction Mechanic 3rd Class Marvin Shields, despite severe wounds, knocked out an enemy machine gun menacing the American defenders and repeatedly risked his life to save others from the advancing Viet Cong. Shields, however, soon died from his wounds. For his extraordinary valor, the man received the Medal of Honor, the first awarded to a SEABEE.

Aside from the dogged resistance of Shields and the other defenders, air support kept the VC from completely seizing the camp. Beginning at dawn on

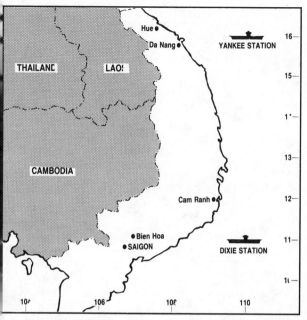

THAILAND • Hue
Da Nang •
LAOS 16—
YANKEE STATION
15—
1'—
13—
CAMBODIA
Cam Ranh •◄ 12—
• Bien Hoa
• SAIGON 11—
DIXIE STATION
1(—
10^ 106 10^ 110

WARM-UP STATION:
Dixie Station, several hundreds of miles to the south of Yankee Station, was used to support operations over South Vietnam. It also doubled as a warm-up station for naval aviators new to the war. Flying missions over South Vietnam, they could get their first taste of combat without facing the twin hazards of SAMs and antiaircraft fire. These they would experience when they were tranferred to Yankee Station and began flying over Laos and North Vietnam.

the 10th and for three days afterwards, US and Vietnamese air force units and squadrons from *Oriskany*'s Carrier Air Wing 16 strafed enemy positions, bombed overrun buildings, and ringed the battle site with fire, killing hundreds of enemy soldiers. Finally, South Vietnamese and American ground forces broke the siege and retook the smoking, blackened ruin that was Dong Xoai.

This aerial assistance to the ground war continued into the fall of 1965 as antisubmarine carrier *Hornet* began a combat tour off South Vietnam. The Essex-class ship carried mostly A-4 Skyhawks and A-1 Skyraiders, the latter especially suited to the air support role.

During all of 1965, Task Force 77 units flew 26,000 attack, reconnaissance, search-and-rescue, and combat air patrol sorties in South Vietnam. The Dixie Station carriers also provided air cover and close air support for the Dagger Thrust amphibious landings on the central Vietnamese coast. Unfortunately, these operations met with little success. In most cases the Viet Cong simply slipped into the jungle in the face of large-scale landings.

The next year witnessed much the same type of activity as the Dixie Station carriers dispatched

Stopping the flow

SEAGOING AIRFIELD: The *Essex*-class carrier *Hornet*, serving as an antisubmarine warfare ship, prepares to launch aircraft for patrol operations in the Gulf of Tonkin. Older carriers, such as *Hornet* operated effectively in Southeast Asia, especially off South Vietnam, as mobile bases for the fleet's smaller planes and helicopters.

their air units to the battlefields of South Vietnam. Naval aviators bombed and strafed Viet Cong forces attempting to drub the South Vietnamese Army before American groundunits joined the war in strength. Naval air support helped to frustrate the enemy's plan.

When *Intrepid* relieved *Hancock* on station in May, she carried no fighters but a heavy complement of attack aircraft. The enemy air threat to Dixie Station carriers was nil and allied ground forces needed all the help they could get. The 32 A-4s and 24 A-1s of Carrier Air Wing 10 added real punch to

he fleet's close air support strikes. By August, the
Navy had flown more than 21,000 combat and combat support sorties in the South.

That same month, US leaders were finally confident that enough US and South Vietnamese air force squadrons were on hand in the Republic of Vietnam to carry out most of the in-country air strikes. As a result, the Navy closed down Dixie Station and sent *Intrepid* north to join *Ranger* and *Constellation* in the Gulf of Tonkin. From August 1966 to the end of the war, the Seventh Fleet launched all air operations over South Vietnam, North

Vietnam, and Laos from one staging area, Yankee Station.

Even though Task Force 77's attention was focused on the war in South Vietnam and North Vietnam during 1965 and 1966, carrier units flew numerous missions in Laos. As part of the continuing Yankee Team program, carrier-based RF-8A and RA-5C photo reconnaissance planes canvassed the jungles of eastern Laos to monitor the flow south of communist troops and supplies.

Early in the war American commanders recognized the special importance of enemy activity in the Laotian panhandle. On April 3, 1965, they divided Laos into two operational areas: Barrel Roll, which encompassed the region north of the Ho Chi Minh Trail; and Steel Tiger, which included the critical infiltration corridor through southern Laos. That November, US leaders further subdivided the southern operational area into Steel Tiger and Tiger Hound. In this sector, adjacent to the Laos-South Vietnamese border, Air Force aerial spotters searched for targets and then called in air strikes by Navy and Air Force attack aircraft.

Location of the vital passes along the Ho Chi Minh Trail bombed by carrier-based units.

In each of these areas, carrier attack planes flew night operations in search of truck convoys, staging sites, and even single supply vehicles. The one or two-plane naval units used parachute flares and other illumination devices to find the skillfully concealed foe. By day, larger carrier forces bombed the constricted Mu Gia, Nape, and Ban Karai passes through the rugged Annam Cordillera of eastern Laos and the roads and bridges feeding the Ho Chi Minh Trail.

Task Force 77 aircraft flew combat sorties in Laos almost every month. But, when the northeast monsoon "socked in" North Vietnam from December through April each year, the carriers at Yankee Station redoubled their efforts in Laos, where flying weather usually was better. The fleet also used the periodic bombing halts in the North to concentrate naval air power on the Ho Chi Minh Trail. For instance, during the month-long bombing pause in January 1966, Task Force 77 aircraft flew more sorties in Laos than they had in the last six months of 1965.

It was on one such mission into the "Elephant Kingdom" of Laos that A-1H pilot Lieutenant (j.g.)

Dieter Dengler made his mark on naval history. While flying over the trail, Dengler's VA 45 Skyraider was knocked out of the sky by intense antiaircraft fire. He crash landed his damaged Skyraider.

The small-built naval aviator, a childhood refugee from war-torn Germany, now began his struggle to survive and escape from his enemies. He initially evaded communist search parties but then was captured and force-marched to a POW compound near Hoi Het. Along the way his captors tortured him. Once in the prison camp, already overflowing with Laotian and Thai men, and Air Force pilot 1st Lieutenant Duane Martin, Dengler was continually mistreated and denied food by his Pathet Lao guards.

For five months he planned his escape. His opportunity came when the prisoners, fearing the Pathet Lao were about to kill them, burst out of their huts. The desperate men overpowered and killed a number of guards and fled into the surrounding jungle.

On duty —During launch and recovery of aircraft from carriers UH-2A Seasprite helicopters were used to stand "plane guard", ready to rescue aviators, who had been forced to bail out into the sea.

For the next three weeks, Dengler, weak from disease and malnutrition, struggled through the steamy hell of southern Laos. When he and his short-time companion, Lieutenant Martin, entered a village in search of food, they were set upon by an angry, machete-wielding tribesman. The man killed the Air Force pilot. In his weakened state, Dengler barely escaped the same fate. He stumbled back into the tropical forest.

To his horror, the aviator discovered that after weeks of struggling through the leech-, mosquito-, and snake-infested jungle he was no more than five miles from the POW camp. Utterly exhausted and starving, Dengler could go no further. He formed an SOS on the ground with rocks and awaited the end. But fortune smiled on him.

An Air Force Skyraider pilot spotted his rock message and called in a rescue helicopter. Dengler's six-month ordeal was over. He was the second—and last—naval aviator to escape from communist captivity during the war in Southeast Asia.

Meanwhile, his comrades had continued to strike enemy supply lines in Laos. Flying 25 percent of the sorties in this joint Navy-Air Force campaign, Task Force 77 air units spent the winter of 1966 and 1967

hitting truck parks, convoys, and single vehicles in "truck busting" operations. Yankee Station A-1 and A-4 attack squadrons also cut and cratered key roads, knocked down bridges, and riddled supply boats in the rivers of the panhandle.

In general, however, targets were hard to find. The jungled and mountainous terrain of eastern Laos, often blanketed with a fine opaque mist, shielded much enemy activity from American aviators.

To help penetrate this shield, in November 1967 the Navy deployed to Nakhon Phanom, Thailand, a special aerial reconnaissance unit, Observation Squadron (VO) 67. The 300-man unit flew the old reliable Neptune patrol plane, extensively modified to accommodate advanced radars, navigational

stems, radios, cameras, and 7.62-millimeter mini-
uns. The new version, designated OP-2E, was also
quipped to drop electronic sensors along the Ho Chi
Iinh Trail to monitor the infiltration traffic.

VO 67 was star-crossed. Several months after the
:art of operations in November 1967, the unit suf-
ered the loss of its executive officer, Commander
elbert A. Olson, his OP-2E aircraft, and the entire
ight-man crew. Flying in foul weather, the pilot
as unable to avoid the cliff face of a mountain when
e pulled up from dropping electronic sensors
apable of detecting enemy ground movement. One
10nth later, in February 1968, the communists hit
nother plane with antiaircraft fire during a low-
vel mission. The naval aviator tried to fly the Nep-

Location of Nakhon Phanom —the Thai airfield served as a base for a naval reconnaissance squadron monitoring movements along the Ho Chi Minh Trail.

tune back to Nakhon Phanom, but he never made it. The plane crashed and burned and all nine crewmen were killed.

Only ten days later, tragedy struck again. Flying low to seed the ground with sensors, an OP-2E crossed over an enemy antiaircraft site. Communist 37-millimeter fire ripped into the plane, killing one man and igniting a blaze. With fire and smoke spreading throughout the aircraft, the brave commander ordered everyone to bail out. He waited until his men had cleared the plane and then he too jumped into the black night. Rescue helicopters soon picked up the seven crewmen but the brave commander had vanished.

These losses convinced naval leaders that the slow prop-driven Neptune was just not suited to the high threat antiaircraft environment of southern Laos. In July 1968, the Navy disestablished VO 67 and returned its planes and men to the United States.

However, the Neptune-equipped squadron had been intended to serve in the sensor-dropping role only until more advanced Navy and Air Force units were prepared to take over the job. The aviators of VO 67 accomplished this mission with courage and resourcefulness.

Other naval air units operating in Laos faced a different problem—operational restrictions, many as stringent as for the air war in North Vietnam.

Washington often dictated what targets to strike and what weapons to use. Further, the air units needed the permission of the US ambassador to Laos, William Sullivan, or the head of the Laotian Air Force to hit military targets near villages or off the main roads. Of course, the communists placed their logistic units as close as they could to the off limit areas.

The enemy also built new roads and bypasses through the jungle, repaired existing routes, dug caves into the mountains, and camouflaged everything. The well-organized and -defended logistic pipeline through southern Laos functioned with increasing effectiveness. Although the American air campaign slowed and diminished the movement south of troops and supplies by forcing the enemy to operate mostly at night and off the main roads, it did not stop the flow. Using bicycles, porters, and pack animals where they had to, North

ietnamese Army (NVA) replacements, heavy
eapons, and ammunition were pushed down the
ail and into South Vietnam.

The reason for the surge of infiltration into the
uth was explained when a number of NVA divi-
ons surrounded and laid siege to the US Marine
se at Khe Sanh, six miles from the Laotian border,
late 1967 and early 1968. US leaders feared a
peat of the Dien Bien Phu disaster of 1954 that
omed the French war effort in Indochina.

To insure the safety of Khe Sanh and to strike
rd at the rarely concentrated enemy forces,
eneral Westmoreland gathered US air power from
l over the Pacific theater. B-52 bombers and other
ir Force units based in Thailand and Guam,
arine units operating from Da Nang and Chu Lai
South Vietnam, and US Navy squadrons flying
om Yankee Station combined in Operation
iagara to pour it on the enemy.

During February and March, Task Force 77 attack
uadrons joined the aerial assault on the besiegers
Khe Sanh. Flying more than 1,500 attack sorties
ch month, naval aircraft rocketed and strafed and
opped napalm bombs on enemy positions, as close
100 yards to the base. The deluge of fire from the
merican aerial armada, especially from the B-52
mbers, each of which carried 30 tons of bombs,
vastated enemy forces. Entire infantry regiments

BLOCKBUSTER:
Ranger
**ordnancemen
gingerly attach
a 2,000-pound
general-
purpose bomb
to the
underside
station of an
A-1 Skyraider.
Other ordnance
carried by the
fleet's attack
planes included
250-, 500-,
750-, and
1,000-pound
bombs and
napalm bombs.**

were wiped out. Finally, against light opposition
allied ground units broke through to the gallant
Marine defenders and lifted the siege.

From the end of the Rolling Thunder campaign
against North Vietnam in November 1968 to early
1972, Task Force 77 concentrated its air squadrons
against Laos and South Vietnam. Combat was
fierce, with 130 naval aircraft and many crews lost.
During that time the Navy dropped 700,000 tons of
ordnance.

However, operations were limited following the
lessened operational commitment and a Navy effort
to cut down on the expenditures on fuel, ammuni-

**ENROUTE
TO TARGET:**
Two heavily-armed A-6A Intruder aircraft from *Constellation* head for targets in Vietnam. The day-night, all-weather jet was the Navy's most versatile attack aircraft. Its advanced navigation and bombing systems enabled precision strikes during the foul weather often experienced in Southeast Asia's monsoon seasons. The Intruder's electronics accounted for 13 percent of its weight and were operated by a bombardier/navigator.

ion, and aircraft. Between 1968 and 1972, general-y two aircraft carriers, rather than three, steamed t Yankee Station.

US leaders kicked off this new era of the Southeast Asian air war in November 1968 with a series of perations in Laos called Commando Hunt. The new dministration of President Richard M. Nixon was nthusiastic about bringing massive air power to ear against the Ho Chi Minh Trail. With the radual withdrawal of American ground forces from outheast Asia, Washington wanted the US air and aval forces to protect the South Vietnamese and aotian allies striving to take on the major burden

Flight control —in the aircraft handling center of the *Bon Homme Richard* scale templates of each aircraft are maneuvered in accordance with their positions on the flight and hangar decks. The handling center was essential to the smooth-running of the ship's 24-hour air operations schedule. Launching, recovering, and moving fueled and bomb-laden aircraft around the crowded deck safely required precise planning.

of the war. Throughout 1969 and 1970, the Yankee Station carriers joined the US Seventh Air Force in plastering the maze-like supply routes in southern Laos. Thousands of trucks were destroyed.

In Operation Commando Bolt, the Navy used the all-weather, day-night A-6 Intruder, the new EA-6B Prowler ECM aircraft, smart bombs, and ground sensors to interdict supply lines at the vital Ban Karai and Mu Gia passes.

The naval air operations in Laos and South Vietnam got a boost when *America* arrived at Yankee Station in May 1970 carrying a squadron of the new A-7E version of the Corsair II. Equipped with improved weapon systems, the A-7E was especially effective in night operations over the Ho Chi Minh Trail. So too was the new A-6C Intruder. This variant sported a cockpit video display that showed targets on the ground. America also embarked detachments of the advanced KA-6D aerial tanker aircraft.

Carrier operations in Laos took on a different form in February 1971, when the South Vietnamese Army (ARVN) launched Operation Lam Son 719. Its best armor, airborne, and ranger units attacked west on Route 9 from the DMZ area as far as Tchepone, across the border in Laos, to disrupt logistic operations along the Ho Chi Minh Trail, long the desire of American and Vietnamese theater commanders.

Supporting the ARVN drive were aircraft units from *Hancock*, *Ranger*, and *Kitty Hawk*. The operation went smoothly at first. But then North Vietnamese forces converged on the area, overrunning one ARVN advance base after another by moving too close to friendly troops for American aircraft to lay down a protective barrier. To make matters worse, flying weather was abysmal and enemy antiaircraft defenses were thick. The mauled South Vietnamese Army withdrew from Laos.

Although the bombing of North Vietnam halted on November 1, 1968, the Navy and the Air Force continued aerial reconnaissance missions. The Navy's RF-8 Crusader and RA-5 Vigilante aircraft supported by fighter escorts, Iron Hand Skyhawks, SAR planes, aerial tankers, and electronic jamming aircraft, flew over the still-dangerous skies.

Only when the North Vietnamese attacked could naval aviators take aggressive action. That occurred

Stopping the flow

LEAPFROG:
An F-4B Phantom of Fighter Squadron 143 launched from the waist catapult of *Ranger* overtakes an A-4 Skyhawk preparing to launch from the port catapult. During combat missions planes were often launched with no more than 15 second intervals.

often enough. By the end of 1970, the joint American
air forces had flown more than 60 "protective reac-
tion" strikes. The following year they flew twice as
many.

Sometimes, North Vietnamese MiGs threatened.
In March 1970, a Constellation F-4J flown by Lieute-
nant Jerome E. Beaulier and his backseater, Lieute-
nant Steven J. Barkley, destroyed a MiG-21 over the
North—the Navy's only aerial victory between
September 1968 and January 1972.

To demonstrate American resolve in Southeast
Asia and to deter a feared communist attack on

Stopping the flow

ON THE CATAPULT: A sleek RA-5C Vigilante is readied for take-off from *Ranger*. The barracuda-like photo reconnaissance plane was equipped with a radar inertial guidance system and automatic flight controls so that it remained precisely on course, even over the most heavily-defended areas of North Vietnam. Photos taken by its technically-advanced cameras accurately pinpointed targets by including longtitude and latitude references in the border of each picture.

outh Vietnam in 1972, President Nixon ordered a ort bombing campaign in the North at the end of 971. The day after Christmas, Navy and Air Force nits began a five-day strike, code-named Proud eep, against fuel and supply depots, truck parks, rfields, and SAM sites below the 20th parallel. The int force flew more than 1,000 sorties.

Proud Deep symbolized a change in the air war. fter three years hitting supply lines and units in outh Vietnam and Laos, the US air forces were gain focusing on the enemy's warmaking nerve enter in North Vietnam.

Air Power Unleashed

6

The Linebacker Offensive 1972

HE Linebacker Offensive during 1972 showed hat US firepower could accomplish against military and industrial nerve centers, if properly handled. For, as never before in the Vietnam War, naval leaders were able to use Seventh Fleet air and surface forces to best advantage.

This climactic episode began with the surprise North Vietnamese assault at the end of March 1972. In contrast to previous campaigns, the Easter Offensive consisted of large-scale tank, artillery, and infantry attacks on regular allied forces. The multidivision army advanced in three areas: across the DMZ, through the Central Highlands, and toward Saigon from Cambodia. The stunned South Vietnamese defenders fell back before the onrushing enemy legions.

With most American ground units withdrawn from South Vietnam, as part of the "Vietnamization" of the war, the US command had only air and naval forces to fall back on. Acting quickly, President Nixon ordered the Pacific Command to help South Vietnam stop and then roll back the North Vietnamese Army.

Seventh Fleet aircraft carriers *Hancock* and *Coral Sea* immediately sent attack squadrons against the NVA divisions advancing on Hue, while ships shelled them from close offshore. Each day, up to 20 cruisers and destroyers armed with 8-inch and 5-inch guns poured fire into the enemy's ranks. On April 6, the fleet extended the battlefield north of the DMZ with strikes against communist supply lines.

Kitty Hawk and *Constellation* steamed from the western Pacific to join their sisters at Yankee Station. In April, carrier air wings from these ships, in

Operation Freedom Train, carried out Alpha strikes on key military and industrial facilities at Vinh, Dong Hoi, and Thanh Hoa.

On the 16th, as B-52 bombers conducted a surprise raid against a POL depot near Hanoi, carrier aircraft destroyed three MiGs on the ground at Kien An airfield and demolished military warehouses near Haiphong. The cruiser *Oklahoma City* and three destroyers leveled enemy installations on Do Son Peninsula, which guarded the river approach to North Vietnam's major port.

Smaller aircraft flights and other cruisers and destroyers attacked transportation routes, troop concentrations, supply depots, and shore defenses the length of the North Vietnamese panhandle.

While these limited operations were effective, the Nixon administration recognized that something more was needed to aid its struggling allies. A resumption of Rolling Thunder-type air strikes was not enough.

The president accepted the advice of his naval advisors, especially that of the hard-nosed JCS chairman, Admiral Thomas H. Moorer, that interdicting the road and rail lines from China and closing the port of Haiphong to imports would take the steam out of the Easter Offensive. Over 85 percent of North Vietnam's imports passed through Haiphong, as did almost all of the munitions that fueled the modern sophisticated war effort; this included the tanks, artillery, and ammunition needed on the southern battlefronts and the SA-2 missiles, MiGs, radars, and antiaircraft artillery essential to the North's air defense.

By the spring of 1972, this defensive arsenal was awesome. Over 300 SAM sites dotted the countryside. Antiaircraft artillery guns numbered 1,500, including many of the high-altitude, radar-guided 85-millimeter and 100-millimeter weapons. The North Vietnamese Air Force deployed an interceptor fleet of 250 aircraft. Command centers tied in with almost 200 radar stations directed the entire defensive network in a coordinated resistance campaign.

On May 5, Nixon ordered final preparations for full-scale bombing and mining campaign. The president and Secretary of State Henry Kissinger decided that the risks of Soviet or Chinese intervention

Adm. Thomas H. Moorer —chairman of the Joint Chiefs of Staff (JCS) during Linebacker. He advised President Nixon on the necessity of bombing North Vietnam's road and rail links with China and mining Haiphong harbor.

were minimal; both communist powers sought better relations with the United States.

The Seventh Fleet marshalled its carrier forces. In addition, the Atlantic Fleet's *Saratoga* embarked Carrier Air Wing 3, took on supplies, and headed for the Pacific. By the 23rd of May, six mighty flattops—*Saratoga*, *Constellation*, *Coral Sea*, *Hancock*, *Kitty Hawk*, and *Midway*—steamed at Yankee Station—the largest concentration of such ships in the war. Almost 500 attack, fighter, and special aircraft could be launched from their decks.

On May 9, even before *Saratoga* reached Southeast Asian waters, her sisters inaugurated the new air campaign. In the early morning light, *Coral Sea* catapulted three A-6 Intruders and six A-7 Corsairs, each armed with four magnetic-acoustic sea mines. Led by Commander Roger Sheets, they split into two groups and headed for Haiphong. The jets skimmed over the water at 50 feet to slide in under radar. Radio silence was absolute.

As Sheets and his comrades closed on the coast, other Seventh Fleet units set up a protective shield. F-4 Phantoms raced ahead to guard against the MiGs based at Phuc Yen and Kep airfields near Hanoi. ECM planes jammed enemy radar. The guided missile cruisers *Chicago* and *Long Beach* steamed to positions 40 miles offshore, from which they could defend the strike group with Talos surface-to-air missiles.

Even before Sheets's attack flight reached the target area, *Chicago*'s radars picked up four aerial contacts approaching fast from the northwest. The cruiser immediately launched several SAMs at the "bogies". Radar operators watched as one blip disappeared from their screens. The other three hostile contacts beat a fast retreat.

Under this defensive umbrella, the mine-laden Intruders and Corsairs reached their target. At 0859, *Coral Sea*'s attack aircraft began dropping their mines along the water approach to Haiphong. In two minutes the jets had planted their ordnance and banked towards the gulf. Not one plane was damaged.

Minutes after Sheets verified the success of this well planned and well-executed operation, code-named Pocket Money, President Nixon announced over radio and television that the United States was

Secretary of State Henry Kissinger —advised President Nixon that there would be only a minimal risk of Soviet and Chinese intervention if the US launched the Linebacker bombing campaign against North Vietnam.

Air Power Unleashed

ALPHA STRIKE: Three F-4 Phantom II aircraft (foreground) from *Midway*'s Fighter Squadron 161 and three A-7E Corsair IIs from *America* drop their bombs during a strike mission over North Vietnam. Because the F-4 was not equipped for accurate level bomb delivery, it flew on bombing missions with a lead-ship, which signalled when to release the bomb load.

instituting an air and naval blockade of North Vietnam. He also revealed that the mines in the Haiphong river approach would not be activated for three days. The president advised the Soviet, Chinese, and Eastern European merchant ships in Haiphong to put to sea while they could. Despite this warning, 31 ships elected to remain trapped in North Vietnamese waters.

In the next few weeks, Task Force 77 laid other minefields in the secondary ports of Hon Gay and Cam Pha and in the river entrances to Quang Khe, Dong Hoi, Thanh Hoa, and Vinh.

From May through December 1972, not one large

erchant vessel entered or left a North Vietnamese
arbor. The communists attempted to lighter cargo
shore from ships in international waters but
eventh Fleet destroyers and aircraft, including
Marine carrier-based helicopter gunships, hunted
own the shuttling craft.

On May 10, Navy and Air Force units began a
rushing air assault. As in Rolling Thunder, three
ears before, the objective remained limited: to com-
el the enemy to negotiate by starving his front-line
orces of logistic support.

However, this new air offensive, called
inebacker, differed in one important respect:

Target of opportunity —an aerial view of two North Vietnamese convoy vehicles destroyed by attacks by aircraft from Attack Squadron 146 aboard *Constellation*. Photo intelligence later identified the trucks as Soviet-built Ural-375s.

Washington now allowed the leaders in the comba theater to run the war. Operational commande decided when, how, and in what order to strike an restrike targets. Air units adjusted their attacks, a cording to the weather and air defenses, to pla maximum firepower on the enemy.

To complement the naval blockade, carrier a units concentrated on the road and rail lines fro China and on warmaking resources, including pow plants, fuel storage facilities, and munitio stockpiles.

In addition to full lockers of conventional "iro bombs," Task Force 77 carriers now held thousanc of precision guided weapons, or smart bombs. Thes included the laser-guided bomb and improved ve sions of the Walleye glide bomb, nicknamed Fa Albert.

The opening day of Linebacker was a blockbuste Navy A-6 Intruders and A-7 Corsairs heavil damaged the Hai Duong railroad yard on th strategic line between Haiphong and the capital

In a daring operation, Seventh Fleet cruise *Newport News* steamed right up to the coastline o Haiphong. Its 8-inch guns shelled targets nea Hanoi while guided missile cruisers *Oklahoma C ty* and *Providence* defended against MiG attack an three destroyers bombarded shore batteries on th Do Son Peninsula. At the same time, Air Force uni dropped the long-standing Paul Doumer Bridge a Hanoi into the Red River.

But the most significant action took place in th skies high above the Tonkin Delta as American an North Vietnamese fighter pilots fought to the deat in one of the largest dogfights of the war. Air Forc units shot down three MiGs, but lost two of their ow Phantoms. Of the 21 communist interceptors tha rose to meet the Navy's fighter escorts, eight r turned to earth in flames.

The seeds of this dramatic Navy victory wer planted years before when the service set up the To Gun school for fighter tactics at Miramar Naval A Station near San Diego. This occurred at the end Rolling Thunder in November 1968. Then nav leaders were concerned over the low two-to-one rat of MiG kills to losses of naval aircraft. At the schoo pilots spent five weeks in class and flying mock ai to-air battles against veteran naval aviato

quipped with A-4 Skyhawks and F-5 Freedom
ighters. These jets were similar in size and
naneuverability to MiG-17 and MiG-21 intercep-
ors. By the end of their course, most pilots were well
ersed in the tactics and flying skills needed for suc-
essful air-to-air combat in Southeast Asia.

Top Gun graduates Lieutenant Randy Cun-
ingham and Lieutenant (j.g.) Willie Driscoll
earned their lessons well. Even before the start of
inebacker, the F-4J Phantom pilot and his RIO of
'onstellation's VF 96 had bagged a MiG-21 and a
1iG-17 with Sidewinders.

But, their time to shine came on that fierce day
f battle, May 10, 1972. That morning "Duke" Cun-
ingham and "Irish" Driscoll began one more day
n the line off North Vietnam. First thing, they went
n deck to observe the ordnance handlers,
naintenance men, catapult operators, and other
ssential crewmen bending their backs to their hard
nd dangerous work. Already the tropical sun and
umidity bore down on these dedicated members of
he carrier team.

After a breakfast of spicy omelets in the flight crew
ness, the two young officers headed for the pre-flight
riefing compartment. The day's mission was to be
strike on the strategic Hai Duong railroad yard
hat was circled by airfields, SAM sites, and "triple
.." Cunningham and Driscoll were assigned the
nission of silencing antiaircraft guns before zoom-
ng skyward to guard against MiG intruders.

For several hours, the aviators tensely awaited
aunch time as they studied aerial photographs of
lefenses and then checked out their aircraft. All was
eady. The aviators climbed into their F-4J with the
adio call sign "Showtime 100". When their turn
ame, Cunningham rolled the Phantom up to posi-
ion at the catapult, fired up his engines, gave the
light deck director the thumbs up sign, and braced
or takeoff. Wham! The jet streaked off *Connie's*
ngled deck at 200 knots. Once he was aloft with
he other "Fighting Falcons" of VF 96, Cunningham
ook on fuel from an aerial tanker and headed for
North Vietnam.

Over the target, the attacking Corsairs and In-
ruders peeled off and dived on the rail yard. Their
,000-pound bombs smothered locomotives, rolling
tock, and tracks in smoke and flame. As Cun-

**First aces
—Lt. Randall
Cunningham
(above) and his
radar intercept
officer, Lt. (j.g.)
William P.
Driscoll,
became the
first American
flight crew to
down five
enemy aircraft.
They had
already downed
a MiG-17 and a
MiG-21 when,
on May 10,
1972, their
Phantom shot
down three
more MiG-17s,
including North
Vietnam's top
ace,
Col. Toon.**

Air Power Unleashed

INTERCEPTOR: An F-4 Phantom II being checked for takeoff. This two-man, highly-maneuverable aircraft served as both a bomber and fighter. Capable of flying at twice the speed of sound, F-4s were frequently the first choice to fly fighter escort to bomber squadrons and provide cover against MiG attacks. The F-4 accounted for sixty percent of the Navy's MiG kills and all those that occurred during 1972.

ningham released his own ordnance, his wingma
called out a warning: MiG-17s were right on th
F-4's tail and firing. Cunningham turned hard t
port and one communist jet overshot the Phantom
The American pilot ripped off one of his fou
Sidewinders. It flew right up the MiG's exhaust an
blew the plane apart.

After that, there was a general melee of MiG-17s
MiG-19s, MiG-21s, and F-4s over Hai Duong. Fly
ing to the assistance of a Phantom with two bogie
on his tail, and another to starboard, Cunningham
fired one more heat-seeker. This one hit home too
An enemy interceptor exploded in flame. The pilo
punched out and Cunningham just missed hitting
him.

Looking around and seeing nothing but a sky full of MiGs, "Duke" Cunningham and his RIO headed for the coast. Before they got there, however, a MiG-17 flew straight at them, his 37-millimeter guns blazing. The American pilot put his plane in a vertical climb to escape the fire; but the MiG stayed right with him and pulled up parallel only 300 feet away. This was no green adversary! Each man looked the other in the face in a silent deadly challenge. The communist pilot was none other than Colonel Toon, North Vietnam's top ace, with 13 American aircraft to his credit.

Cunningham pulled his jet over the top, ignited his afterburner, and headed down. Toon fired at the F-4 as it passed and jumped in behind the diving

141

Aerial interdiction —Linebacker continued the attack on enemy supply lines. Here the span of a bridge near Duong Phuong Thuong lies collapsed in the river after a strike by aircraft from *Hancock*.

fighter. As the two jets descended, first one and then the other would gain the tail position, but not long enough to make a kill.

Both aircraft broke out of this pattern and into a near vertical climb once again. Then, Cunningham tried a different tactic. He throttled back and put on the speed brakes. The F-4 slowed to 150 knots and the MiG streaked past. At this point the American was too close to use an air-to-air missile. Then Toon ended his climb and headed for the deck. Cunningham came in right behind him and squeezed off his third Sidewinder. It hit the MiG which began trailing black smoke and gradually headed down. The brave and skillful Colonel Toon and his aircraft soon plunged into the ground. Cunningham and Driscoll now were the first American aces of the Vietnam War.

Almost immediately, angry MiG-17s jumped on the Phantom's tail while others approached from the front. Evading these adversaries, "Showtime 100" again made for the coast. Suddenly, an SA-2 Guideline surface-to-air missile exploded to the front of the F-4.

The damaged plane soon began to fly erratically and burn. The pilot had all he could do to coax it out over the water. Within seconds of making "feet wet," all systems failed and the F-4 spun toward the drink. At the last moment Cunningham and Driscoll punched out of their doomed fighter.

As the two aviators parachuted down calling out "Mayday, Mayday" on their survival radios, their comrades pounced on enemy patrol boats and other vessels hoping to capture the pair. Soon after the downed fliers landed in the water and climbed into their life rafts, three Marine SAR helicopters from *Oriskany* retrieved them from these inhospitable waters at the mouth of the Red River. The two aces were greeted as heroes when a helicopter returned them to their cheering shipmates thronging *Connie*'s flight deck.

If this demonstration of aerial prowess was not a clear indication that the Navy had trained its fighter pilots well, by the end of American combat operations over North Vietnam on January 15, 1973, the conclusion was inescapable: Task Force 77's ratio of MiG kills to losses during the Linebacker campaign stood at twelve to one.

Air Power Unleashed

AT THE READY: *Constellation*'s Phantom, Vigilante, and Corsair aircraft stand in readiness on May 9, 1972 to inaugurate a hard-hitting air campaign against the North Vietnamese, whose Easter Offensive against South Vietnam had gravely threatened the allied position. Following the mining and closure of Haiphong on that day, Task Force 77 kicked off the massive Linebacker II bombing operation that helped to stop the enemy's ground push and to bring his negotiators to the peace table.

While the "fighter jocks" were racking up this im
pressive score, their Navy and Marine Corps com
rades in the attack squadrons brought the enemy'
war machine to a grinding halt. Between May 9 an
the end of September, Task Force 77 units flew a
average of 4,000 day and night attack sorties eac
month. In August it peaked at over 4,700 sorties

The Intruder, Corsair, and Skyhawk squadron
flew multi-aircraft Alpha strikes and smaller mis
sions against key targets, such as the seemingly in
destructible Dragon's Jaw bridge at Thanh Hoa. O
May 13, the Air Force finally dropped a large sec

TRIPLE ACTION: Snub-nosed Corsair IIs, based on *Kitty Hawk*, streak towards Viet Cong targets in South Vietnam. The Corsair II was used extensively for daylight tactical missions during Linebacker. They carried two 20mm cannon in the nose and two fuselage pylons that allowed the subsonic attack plane to deliver a weapon load of 15,000 pounds.

tion of the bridge with smart bombs. Navy and Air Force strikes kept it closed to communist traffic for the rest of the war.

The American air forces knocked down most of the major bridges between the Chinese border and the Tonkin Delta and from there south into the panhandle. The aerial offensive also left no segment of the North Vietnamese rail system longer than 50 miles uncut. More and more, the enemy relied on slower and less efficient truck transport.

Compounding all of the enemy's logistic woes was the gradual drying up of fuel supplies. The closure

Air Power Unleashed

BLOWN APART: A span of the railroad and highway bridge over the Day River at Ninh Binh lies under water after *Kitty Hawk* aircraft dropped an advanced Walleye glide bomb on the target in July 1972. This and other precision-guided munitions used during the Linebacker campaign significantly improved accuracy. The famous Dragon's Jaw bridge at Thanh Hoa, which withstood three years of American attack, finally fell to USAF "smart bombs" on May 13, 1972.

of Haiphong to Soviet tankers, the destruction of the POL pipeline north and south of the Red River Delta, and the leveling of major fuel storage facilities brought this about. By the end of September, reserves of POL were extremely low and scattered throughout the war-torn country. The Navy-Air Force assault forced the communists to use up more of their precious fuel on diesel-powered electrical generators by shutting down most primary power plants.

The concentrated and increasingly devastating Linebacker campaign helped to stall the communist Easter Offensive in South Vietnam. Its tank-, artillery-, and vehicle-heavy invasion army required much more logistic support than the guerrilla forces in past drives. The communists did not get the support they needed to win. In addition, the South Vietnamese armed forces, backed up by US air power, stopped the communist offensive and then retook lost ground.

President Richard M. Nixon —ordered the massive Linebacker II bombing campaign after peace talks collapsed.

With their big push of 1972 a failure, the communists suddenly became more amenable at the peace negotiations in Paris. Sensing the possibility of a political solution to the war, President Nixon, on October 23, restricted bombing to targets below the 20th parallel. Secretary of State Kissinger announced that "peace is at hand".

Of course, the enemy continued his "talk/fight" strategy by rebuilding the transportation system, stiffening defenses, and restocking war supplies. In the absence of military pressure, the North Vietnamese negotiators became more and more obstinate. In mid-December the Paris talks collapsed when the communist diplomats walked out. President Nixon's ultimatum that they return to the conference table—or else—was scorned.

Throughly exasperated, Nixon ordered a massive, no holds barred campaign, code-named Linebacker II, against North Vietnam's warmaking heart. On the night of December 18, and for many nights thereafter, waves of B-52 bombers hit targets right in Hanoi. Other Air Force tactical units and Task Force 77 squadrons struck command-communications facilities, power plants, rail yards, storage buildings, bridges, supply depots, truck parks, and ship repair complexes in Hanoi and Haiphong.

The enemy sent up a barrage of SAMs that

PICKET DUTY: *Hancock*'s flight deck personnel ready an E1-B Tracer aircraft for catapulting off the angled-deck carrier. These odd-looking planes, flying at 30,000 feet and carrying 11,000 pounds of electronic gear, served as advanced radar pickets. They warned of attacking MiGs, directed American aircraft to targets, and acted as airborne radio relay stations. The pancake-like radar dome was later replaced with a more streamlined version.

brought down a number of the heavy bombers, six on December 20 alone. During the short Linebacker II siege, SA-2s destroyed 15 B-52s and three supporting aircraft. AAA and MiGs got another four Navy planes.

Worried about the initial heavy bomber losses over Hanoi, air commanders concentrated aerial firepower on the missile defense system, including radar and command facilities, missile assembly and transportation stations, and the SA-2 batteries themselves. Using advanced ECM and target finding gear and smart weapons, US forces overcame the enemy defenses. Simultaneously, the Navy and the

Air Force spread the enemy thin by striking targets at Long Dun Kep, Thai Nguyen, Lang Dang, and Haiphong. On the final day of Linebacker II, December 29, the North's "flying telephone poles" were almost all used up and there were no re-placements. American aircraft losses were minimal.

Linebacker II brought the North Vietnamese back to the conference table, where they stayed. Cease-fire conditions were agreed to. On January 15, 1973, the bloody air war over North Vietnam was ended.

On the 27th, US, South Vietnamese, North Viet-namese, and Viet Cong officials signed the Paris cease-fire agreement. The United States agreed to

sweep all mines from North Vietnamese ports and inland waterways and to withdraw its remaining military forces from the South. In exchange, the communists promised to release all American prisoners of war.

During the next two months, 138 naval aviators were flown to freedom aboard American aircraft. Among their number was Lieutenant Commander Everett Alvarez, Jr., who had been in captivity since August 1964.

In Operation Homecoming, the Navy gave the men complete medical, psychological, and emotional support for the often-difficult transition to stateside life. Other Navy POWs were not as fortunate: 36

EVACUATION:
An Air Force HH-53 helicopter prepares to land and disembark refugees on *Midway*'s flight deck in April 1975. The need for a US Marine guard became apparent the previous month when other US ships took on panic-stricken, desperate, and sometimes armed refugees fleeing Da Nang and other cities further north along the coast. By early May, with South Vietnam overrun, the carrier force embarked the last refugees and finally steamed from South Vietnam's coastal waters.

aviators died in captivity, many as a result of the torture from their bestial prison masters. Another 600 pilots and crewmen were missing, presumed dead.

As agreed to at Paris, by March 29, 1973, all American military personnel, with the exception of the US Embassy staff, had departed South Vietnam. Further, from February to July 1973, in Operation End Sweep, 47 minesweepers, amphibious assault ships, and other Seventh Fleet surface units deployed off the communist mainland. Under Task Force 78, naval vessels and helicopters pulling minesweeping sleds and other devices swept North Vietnamese waters clear of the mines that so effectively helped the United States end its direct role in the war.

However, the last act in the long Southeast Asian drama was yet to play. From 1973 to 1975 the South Vietnamese struggled on against the communists without the shield of American air and naval power.

Finally, in March 1975, with US military aid dwindling and the South Vietnamese society disintegrating from its inherent weaknesses, communist forces dealt the Republic of Vietnam the coup de grace. After a local defeat in the Central Highlands, panic swept through the South Vietnamese armed forces and they abandoned one vital region after another. The North Vietnamese Army exploited their foe's disarray and swept south down the coast of South Vietnam until only Saigon and the Mekong Delta remained unoccupied.

As they had been since the birth of the Republic of Vietnam 20 years before, the US Navy's carrier forces were on hand for its demise in April 1975. As communist divisions converged on Saigon, the Navy marshalled Seventh Fleet forces off the South Vietnamese coast. *Enterprise* and *Coral Sea* provided air cover for Task Force 76 amphibious ships, for *Hancock* and *Midway*, which temporarily embarked Navy, Marine, and Air Force helicopters for the evacuation, and for a flotilla of Military Sealift Command merchant ships.

With the defenses of Saigon collapsing on April 29, US leaders ordered the start of Operation Frequent Wind, the evacuation of Americans and close Vietnamese allies. At 1244, *Hancock* launched the first wave of evacuation helicopters from a position 17 miles off the Vung Tau Peninsula. A little over two hours later these aircraft descended into the compound of the US Defense Attache Office in Saigon and began lifting out thousands of evacuees. By 2100 the site was cleared.

Things did not go so easily at the US Embassy downtown. There, thousands of panicking Vietnamese climbed over fences and pressed the Marine perimeter force to get out of the doomed city. American helicopters continued through the night shuttling refugees out to sea. The aircraft had to dodge ground fire along the escape route. Early on the morning of April 30, US Ambassador Graham Martin, over 2,000 evacuees, and the Marine securi-

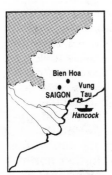

Location of the *Hancock* during the evacuation of refugees from Saigon.

y troops boarded the last helicopters out. Only a few hours later, communist tanks smashed down the gates at the nearby Presidential Palace. Saigon had fallen.

The scene at sea was one of frenzy. Fleeing Vietnamese military aircraft, loaded with fighting men and their families, attempted to land on US carrier decks or ditched alongside. The ships took on 41 helicopters and one trainer but sailors were forced to throw another 54 aircraft over the side to make room.

At the same time Vietnamese Navy vessels, civilian commercial craft, and fishing junks spewed out of the Saigon River and made for the evacuation flotilla.

Finally, on May 2, after days of hectic efforts to embark and care for the 80,000 Vietnamese and American evacuees, the unhappy armada of Vietnamese Navy, Military Sealift Command, and Seventh Fleet combatants sailed for the Philippines and Guam. Flying overhead cover for this allied fleet were the aircraft squadrons of *Hancock*, *Coral Sea*, and *Enterprise*.

Thus ended the carrier Navy's heroic participation in America's long, unsuccessful struggle to preserve the independence of the Republic of Vietnam.

ACNO	— Assistant Chief of Naval Operations.
ARVN	— Army of Vietnam.
ASW	— Antisubmarine Warfare.
BEQ	— Bachelor Enlisted Quarters.
BLT	— Battalion Landing Team.
BOQ	— Bachelor Officers Quarters.
CARDIV	— Carrier Division.
CBPAC	— Naval Construction Battalions US Pacific Fleet.
CBU	— Cluster Bomb Unit.
CG	— Commanding General.
CHICOM	— Chinese communists.
CHJCS	— Chairman of the Joint Chiefs of Staff.
CIA	— Central Intelligence Agency.
CIC	— Combat Information Center.
CICV	— Combined Intelligence Center Vietnam.
CIDG	— Civilian Irregular Defense Group.
CINC	— Commander in Chief.
CINCLANTFLT	— Commander in Chief, US Atlantic Fleet.
CINCPACFLT	— Commander in Chief, US Pacific Fleet.
CL	— Light Cruiser.
CNA	— Center for Naval Analyses.
CNO	— Chief of Naval Operations.
CO	— Commanding Officer.
COM7FLT	— Commander Seventh Fleet.
COMUSMACV	— Commander US Military Assistance Command, Vietnam.
CTF	— Commander Task Force.
CTG	— Commander Task Group.
CTU	— Commander Task Unit.
CV	— Aircraft Carrier.
CVA	— Attack Aircraft Carrier.
CVE	— Escort Aircraft Carrier.
CVW	— Attack Carrier Air Wing.

Glossary

CNO	— Deputy Chief of Naval Operations.
DMZ	— Demilitarized Zone.
DNI	— Director of Naval Intelligence.
DOD	— Department of Defence.
DRV	— Democratic Republic of Vietnam.
ECM	— Electronic Countermeasures.
Flag Plot	— Naval Command Center, Washington.
FMFPAC	— Fleet Marine Force, US Pacific Fleet.
FPB	— Fast Patrol Boat.
GVN	— Government of South Vietnam.
HMM	— Marine Medium Helicopter Squadron.
HMR	— Marine Medium Helicopter Squadron.
HMR	— Marine Transport Helicopter Squadron.
HQ	— Headquarters.
HQ	— Vietnamese Navy (derived from the Vietnamese Hai Quan).
HSAS	— Headquarters Support Activity, Saigon.
JCS	— Joint Chiefs of Staff.
JRC	— Joint Reconnaissance Center.
LCM	— Landing Craft, Mechanized.
LCU	— Landing Craft, Utility.
LCVP	— Landing Craft, Vehicle and Personnel.
LST	— Landing Ship, Tank.
LVT	— Landing Vehicle, Tracked.
MAAG	— Military Assistance Advisory Group.
MACV	— Military Assistance Command, Vietnam.
MAG	— Marine Aircraft Group.
MAW	— Marine Aircraft Wing.
MEB	— Marine Expeditionary Brigade.
MiG	— Russian-made Fighter Aircraft.

NVA	— North Vietnamese Army.
PACFLT	— US Pacific Fleet.
POL	— Petroleum, Oil, Lubricants.
POW	— Prisoner of War.
PSYWAR	— Psychological Warfare.
PT	— Motor Torpedo Boat.
PTF	— Fast Patrol Boat.
R and R	— Rest and Recuperation.
RVAH	— Reconnaissance Attack Squadron.
RVN	— Republic of Vietnam.
RVNAF	— Republic of Vietnam Armed Forces.
SAR	— Search and Rescue.
SEABEE	— Naval Construction Battalion Personnel.
SEAL	— Naval Commando.
SEATO	— Southeast Asia Treaty Organization.
SERE	— Survival, Evasion, Resistance and Escape.
SS	— Steamship.
TF	— Task Force.
USMC	— US Marine Corps.
USN	— US Navy.
USS	— United States Ship.
VA	— Attack Squadron.
VAP	— Heavy Photographic Squadron.
VAW	— Carrier Airborne Early Warning Squadron.
VC	— Viet Cong.
VCP	— Composite Photographic Squadron.
VF	— Fighter Squadron.
VFP	— Light Photographic Squadron.
VMA	— Marine Attack Squadron.
VMF	— Marine Fighter Squadron.
VNAF	— Vietnamese Air Force.
VNN	— Vietnamese Navy.
VP	— Patrol Squadron.

Bibliography

Boyne, Walter J. *Phantom in Combat.* Washington: Smithsonian Institution Press, 1985.

Cagle, Malcolm W. "Task Force 77 in Action off Vietnam." *US Naval Institute Naval Review. Volume 98 (May 1972).*

Cunningham, Randy with Ethell, Jeff. *Fox Two.* Mesa, Az: Champlin Fighter Museum 1984.

Kilduff, Peter. *Douglas A-4 Skyhawk.* London: Osprey Publishing, 1983.

Lavalle, A.J.C., ed. *A Tale of Two Bridges and the Battle for the Skies over North Vietnam.* Washington: US Air Force,1976.

Marolda, Edward J. and Fitzgerald, Oscar P. *From Military Assistance to Combat, 1959-1965.* Vol. II in series, *The United States Navy and the Vietnam Conflict.* Washington: US Naval Historical Center, 1986.

Marolda, Edward J. and G. Wesley Pryce,III. *A Short History of the United States Navy and the Southeast Asian Conflict, 1950-1975.* Washington: US Naval Historical Center, 1984.

Mersky, Peter B. and Polmar, Norman. *The Naval Air war in Vietnam.* Annapolis: The Nautical and Aviation Publishing Company of America, 1981.

Morrocco, John. *Rain of Fire: Air War, 1969-1973.* Boston Publishing Company, 1985.

Morrocco, John. *Thunder From Above: Air War, 1961-1968.* Boston: Boston Publishing Company, 1984.

Stockdale, Jim and Sybil. *In Love and War : The Story of a Family's Ordeal and Sacrifice During the Vietnam Years.* New York: Harper and Rowe, 1984.

Tillman, Barrett. *MiG Master: The Story of the F-8 Crusader.* Annapolis: The Nautical and Aviation Publishing Company of America, 1980.

About
the Author

Edward J. Marolda

The author, Edward J. Marolda is a militar
historian specializing in naval history. He had on
tour in Vietnam from 1969 to 1970, when he serve
as a 1st Lieutenant commanding combat resuppl
convoys in the US Army's 7th Transportatio
Battalion.

He is the coauthor of *From Military Assistance t
Combat, 1959-1965,* Volume II in the official serie
The United States Navy and the Vietnam Conflic
and several other recent histories recording th
Navy's role in Vietnam. He is currently Head of th
Contemporary History Branch of the US Nava
Historical Center in Washington, which he joine
as a historian in 1971.

A graduate of Pennsylvania Military College an
Georgetown University, he has contributed t
military magazines and given lectures on nava
history. He lives in Dale City, Virginia.

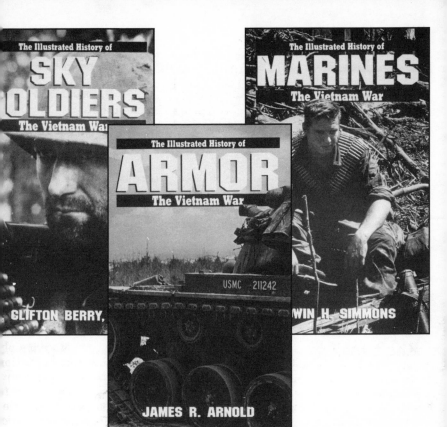

THE ILLUSTRATED HISTORY OF THE VIETNAM WAR

antam's Illustrated History of the Vietnam War is a unique and new series of books exploring in depth the war that seared America to the core: a war that cost 58,022 American lives, that saw great heroism and resourcefulness mixed with terrible destruction and tragedy.

The Illustrated History of the Vietnam War examines exactly what happened: every significant aspect—the physical details, the operations and the strategies behind them—is analyzed in short, crisply written original books by established historians and journalists.

Some books are devoted to key battles and campaigns, others unfold the stories of elite groups and fighting units, while others focus on the role of specific weapons and tactics.

Each volume is totally original and is richly illustrated with photographs, line drawings, and maps.